Supra

Supra

A Feast of Georgian Cooking

Tiko Tuskadze
of Little Georgia

PAVILION

Pavilion
An imprint of HarperCollinsPublishers
1 London Bridge Street
London SE1 9GF

www.harpercollins.co.uk

HarperCollinsPublishers
Macken House
39/40 Mayor Street Upper
Dublin 1
D01 C9W8
Ireland

10 9 8

First published in Great Britain by
Pavilion, an imprint of HarperCollinsPublishers Ltd 2022

ISBN 978-1-91121-616-2

This book contains FSC™ certified paper and other controlled sources to ensure responsible forest management.

For more information visit: www.harpercollins.co.uk/green

Printed in Malaysia

Photography: Yuki Sugiura, Clive Crotty, Zaira Chantladze, Nina Anjaparidze
Design: Laura Russell, Sophie Yamamoto
Illustration: Tamara Melikishvili
Food Stylist: Valerie Berry, Alex James Gray
Editor: Krissy Mallett, Katie Cowan, Stephanie Milner

Contents

Introduction

Georgia is a country built on traditions and of these food is perhaps the most important. Family life revolves around the dining table, and when I was growing up, my family, especially on my father's side, took their food very seriously indeed. My grandmother was like a kitchen magician, conjuring up unforgettably delicious food from the ingredients available to her — she used seasonal ingredients, even through the difficult times when the food supply was erratic. But no matter what challenges she faced, there was always something delicious on the table and plenty to go around, even if friends and neighbours came by unannounced, as they often did. It has become a cliché to talk about one's grandmother, but the reality is that she fostered a love of food and entertaining in me that has remained with me throughout my life and made me the person that I am.

The memory of my life in Georgia is so intense and such an irreplaceable part of me that familiar smells can instantly take me back to my early childhood; the smells of the seasons and of seasonal food are also the smells of my youth. Leaving these memories behind and coming to another country felt like I was a traveller in a physical body leaving her spirit behind.

Luckily, I had the opportunity to open my restaurant, Little Georgia, in London. Within its walls I have created a little homeland and can bring these never-forgotten senses from my old home to my new one. As I mentioned, eating together is a big part of family life in Georgia. Our families are very large and very close, with distant cousins counting as very close relations. We love parties so much that we can always find a reason to celebrate. If a neighbour's cousin's dog had a puppy we would laugh and celebrate with a feast until dawn.

This love for entertaining and the spontaneity of celebration is hard to come by in London. In Georgia, the door was always open and our house was always full of guests, laughing, singing and debating around a table which was groaning under the weight of seemingly endless dishes. These parties were not planned; they just happened and yet there was always food and drink to satisfy the appetite of every impromptu visitor.

I can remember so clearly, as if I had just heard it a moment ago, the comments that our guests made about the food we served them. Even simple salads made by my grandmother were very special. Looking back, I understand now that what was motivating her was a love of watching people enjoying her food, as much as I loved watching her in the kitchen.

Writing this book has brought back so many memories. *Supra* or 'feast', is an integral part of our culture. I cannot escape the memories that flow in my mind from back home of when with nature waking up in spring time the people also seemed to come alive — late night parties, with loud singing, in their gardens. My balcony overlooked the garden of a famous Georgian comedian and actor who had a wooden hut in his garden where he would entertain his guests with parties until sunrise. The smell of baking and barbecue, and the raucous sounds of singing and toasting would waft up through my open windows. Famous poets reciting their works and telling stories, real stories, to a captive and respectful audience. These were not just parties, but celebrations of life — all that is fine about it — in a traditional, dignified and always philosophical manner. When I listened to these people speak, their words were pervaded with wisdom and grace that helped to shape me as a person. If asked what was the smell of my country, I would say spring. And what does spring smell like? Joy. The feeling of eternity and the nonexistence of sorrow.

For me, these memories are a big bottle of love that guides me through misery, grief and hard times. Love is the strongest weapon I was given by my family and it is the strongest weapon that you can hold. I have been very fortunate to have all this and through this book, I hope to share it with you.

The Elements of a *Supra*

Before you start cooking any of the recipes from this book, it is important to understand the ethos and intention behind a traditional Georgian *supra*. One thing that I have struggled with when writing these recipes is dictating how many people each recipe will serve. This is because traditionally each of these dishes is just a small part of a never-ending conveyor belt of delicious dishes that are served at a groaning table during a meal that lasts many hours. If you have prepared a couple of starters(appetizers), a main course and a side dish, then you should have more than enough food to serve 4–6 people. If you've decided to go the whole hog and invite all of your friends and family, then you need to fill the table with small dishes that people can graze on over the course of the evening, refilling empty dishes as you go. This may sound like a lot of work (and it is), but many traditional Georgian dishes, especially the cold salads, use walnut paste as a base, so making up a big batch is a great starting point. The salads can also be made ahead and left in the fridge until an hour or so before you want to serve them, taking the pressure off the host when it comes to getting the meal on the table. Preparing ahead not only relieves some of the pressure on the cook, but also allows the flavours of the fragrant spices (coriander, marigold and fenugreek) that are synonymous with Georgian cuisine time to meld and develop.

Georgian hospitality is legendary the world over and *supra* is at the centre of this generosity of spirit. When hosting a *supra*, you are sharing everything you have — your home, your food, your wine, but also conversation. *Supra* is a coming together over food, but also a meeting of minds and ideas, and central to this is the *tamada*.

Top left and bottom: Music is central to any *supra* with guests joining in with the singing and bringing their own instruments to the celebration.

Top right: A traditional *supra* table laden with dishes. The meals can last for many hours and plates of food are continuously replenished throughout.

Middle left: The toastmaster or *tamada* is the most important guest at a Supra. They lead the toasts and encourage the other guests with laughter and song. They are selected from among the host's family and friends and are pivotal to the success of the celebration.

The *Tamada*

Every *supra* is led by a *tamada* or toastmaster. This is not necessarily the host but someone chosen by the group who is known for their gregarious nature, quick wit and intelligence. It is the job of the *tamada* to lead both the toasts and conversation at a *supra*. The toasts at a *supra* will always start with a toast to Georgia itself, with the toastmaster thanking the land for its bounty and the food at the table. Other speeches will focus on the guests at the table and family and friends now deceased. Only the *tamada* can propose a toast, but other guests are encouraged to respond with their own toasts which can take the form of traditional speeches, jokes, songs or poems. Guests are encouraged to drain their wine glasses with each speech (although this is by no means compulsory), which can lead to good-natured ribbing of the *tamada* as the evening develops.

When I was a child, I have to admit that I found the speeches boring. While the toastmaster was speaking we had to be quiet, which is a struggle for a small child with a lot to say, and I did not always understand what was being discussed. However, as I grew up I came to love and appreciate these speeches and believe that the thoughts and ideas shared within them helped to shape who I am. It is rare in this day and age that the young take the time to listen to the wisdom of their elders, and I cherish these memories and what they gave me.

The Procession of Dishes

Simple salads are the first thing at the table, often laid out before your guests sit down. As well as these, the table will have plates of radishes, tomatoes, salty cheeses and plain bread for people to eat. These salads are never cleared and are refilled as the meal progresses, but successive waves of food are then added to the table. Smaller hot dishes follow cold ones, and then *Khachapuri* (breads, see pages 78–85) are served. These breads are very filling, so it is best to warn those who are unfamiliar with this style of eating that there is more food to come! Meat and vegetable dishes follow and there are always bowls of *Tkemali* (Plum Sauce, see page 22) and *Ajika* (chilli pastes, see pages 28–31) at every table so that people can spice their food themselves. Dessert tends to be simpler, but a cake or *Pelamushi* (Grape Jellies, see page 200) is often served to close the meal.

Wine

It is a matter of pride for a Georgian host that none of their guests has a glass that is more than half empty. Wine is central to a traditional Georgian feast and it is easy to see why — the history of Georgia and the history of wine are intertwined. Georgia is said to be the first place in the world that grapes where cultivated to make wine. Centuries of experience have refined the processes, but traditional wine in Georgia is made in much the same way as it always has been. If you are attending a *supra* in the countryside, the chances are that your hosts make their own wine which will be a source of great pride to them. Homemade wine is stored in large clay vessels called *qvevri* and if the wine at the table never seems to run out, the chances are that it is being drawn from one of these throughout the evening. Georgian wine is gaining popularity the world over and can easily be sourced from a good wine shop or online if you want to serve something really authentic at your feast.

Music

Georgian music and songs are central to a *supra* and, like the toasts, songs to God, peace, the motherland, long life, love, friendship and other topics are proposed. The whole table will join in with the singing and renditions often get louder and more boisterous as more wine is consumed. Often dancing and the playing of instruments accompanies the singing and guests will bring their instruments to dinner for this purpose. At Little Georgia, we often play music by these artists and you can easily find their songs to listen to at home: Hamlet Gonashvili, Debi Ishxnelebi, Inola Gurgulia, the Tsisperi Trio, Kelaptari and Quintet Urmuli.

Pâtés & Sauces

-CHAPTER 1-

Ispanakhis Pkhali
-SPINACH PÂTÉ-

Preparation time: 10 minutes
Cooking time: 5 minutes
Serves 4–6 as part of a *supra*

1 kg/2 lb 3 oz fresh spinach
200 g/7 oz/scant 1¾ cups chopped
    walnuts
3 garlic cloves
1 tsp ground coriander
1 tsp ground marigold
½ tsp hot chilli powder, or to taste
½ tbsp apple cider vinegar or white
    wine vinegar
½ tsp vegetable or sunflower oil
1 bunch spring onions (scallions),
    green parts only, finely sliced
1 handful fresh coriander (cilantro),
    leaves chopped
sea salt, to taste
walnut oil or seeds from
    1 pomegranate, to garnish

Walnuts are synonymous with Georgian cuisine and, when pulsed to a fine paste and flavoured with the classic spice mix *suneli*, form the basis of many classic dishes. Far from being repetitive, walnuts bring a comforting richness to the dishes they are used in but still allow the main ingredients to shine. This spinach and walnut paste makes an excellent accompaniment to bread as part of an elaborate first course at a *supra*, but it is also equally delicious spooned from the bowl and enjoyed in its own right. (Pictured, bottom-left on page 16.)

Bring a large pan of water to the boil, then reduce to a simmer and add the spinach. Cook for 1 minute, until wilted, then drain the spinach through a colander and set aside to cool. Once cool enough to handle, pick up the spinach with your hands and squeeze out any excess water. Place the spinach on a chopping board and chop finely. Transfer to a large bowl and set aside.

Place the walnuts in a food processor and process to a very fine paste. The paste should be sticky and smooth, but not at all grainy (this can take up to 5 minutes).

Crush the garlic with the back of a knife and then put in a mortar with a pinch of sea salt. Grind with a pestle to a smooth paste.

Place the walnut and garlic pastes in a bowl with the ground coriander, ground marigold, chilli powder and vinegar. Using your hands, bring the mixture together to a smooth, thick paste. The paste should be a similar texture to a loose hummus, so add a few drops of water if it is too thick. Set aside.

Place the oil in frying pan (skillet) over a medium heat. Once hot, add the sliced spring onions (scallions) and fry, stirring continuously, until just starting to turn brown, around 2 minutes. Add the fresh coriander (cilantro) to the pan and cook, stirring, for another minute. Add the spring onion and coriander mixture to the bowl with the spinach.

Pour the walnut paste over the top of the spinach and onion mixture, then use your hands to bring everything together until well combined. I like to pick up the mixture in my hands and throw it down into the bowl to encourage the flavours to meld together.

Place the mixture on a serving platter and spread out over the surface with the back of a spoon. Drizzle over some walnut oil and serve. Alternatively, make a small nest from the mixture and serve garnished with fresh pomegranate seeds. This can also be made ahead and refrigerated until ready to serve.

Prasis Pkhali

-LEEK PÂTÉ-

Preparation time: 25 minutes
Cooking time: 20 minutes
Serves 4–6 as part of a *supra*

2 kg/4 lb 6 ½ oz leeks, washed and
    sliced lengthways
100 g/3 ½ oz celery leaves
300 g/10 ½ oz/generous 2 ½ cups
    chopped walnuts
3 garlic cloves
2 tsp ground coriander
2 tsp ground marigold
2 tsp ground blue fenugreek
½ tsp hot chilli powder, or to taste
2 tbsp apple cider vinegar or white
    wine vinegar
2 tsp vegetable or sunflower oil
1 bunch spring onions (scallions),
    white parts only, finely sliced
1 small bunch fresh coriander
    (cilantro), leaves chopped
sea salt and chilli powder, to taste
seeds from 1 pomegranate, to garnish

This delicately flavoured paste brings the subtle flavours of leek and celery to the fore. Like many of the cold dishes in this section, this can be made ahead and removed from the fridge to come down to room temperature just before serving — not only does this allow the flavours time to develop, but also takes some of the pressure off when preparing the many dishes required for a *supra*. (Pictured, top-left on page 16.)

Bring a large pan of water to the boil, then reduce to a simmer and add the leeks. Cook for 5 minutes, then add the celery leaves and cook for 10 minutes more. Drain through a colander and set aside to cool. Once cool enough to handle, pick up the leeks and celery with your hands and squeeze out any excess water.

For best results, I like to pass the leeks and celery through a mincing (meat grinding) machine, but if you do not have one you can use a blender or food processor. Mince/process/blend or roughly chop the leeks and celery to a coarse paste, transfer to a large bowl and set aside.

Place the walnuts in a food processor and process to a very fine paste. The paste should be sticky and smooth, but not at all grainy (this can take up to 5 minutes).

Crush the garlic with the back of a knife and then put in a mortar with a pinch each of sea salt and chilli powder. Grind with a pestle to a smooth paste.

Place the walnut and garlic pastes in a bowl with the ground coriander, marigold, fenugreek, chilli powder and vinegar. Using your hands, bring the mixture together to a smooth, thick paste. The paste should be a similar texture to a loose hummus, so add a few drops of water if it is too thick. Set aside.

Place the oil in frying pan (skillet) over a medium heat. Once hot, add the sliced spring onions (scallions) and fry, stirring continuously, until just starting to turn brown, around 2 minutes. Add the fresh coriander (cilantro) to the pan and cook, stirring, for another minute. Add the spring onion and coriander mixture to bowl with the leeks.

Pour the walnut paste over the top of the leek and onion mixture, then use your hands to bring everything together until well combined.

Place the mixture on a serving platter and spread out over the surface with the back of a spoon. Scatter over the pomegranate seeds and serve.

Jarkhlis Pkhali

-BEETROOT PÂTÉ-

Preparation time: 15 minutes
Cooking time: up to 1 hour 30
   minutes (if using fresh beetroot)
Serves 4–6 as part of a *supra*

1 kg/2 lb 3 oz fresh or cooked beetroot
   (beets)
200 g/7 oz/scant 1¾ cups chopped
   walnuts
3 garlic cloves
1 tsp ground coriander
1 tsp ground marigold
½ tsp hot chilli powder, or to taste
2 tbsp apple cider vinegar or white
   wine vinegar
sea salt and freshly ground black
   pepper
1 handful fresh coriander (cilantro),
   leaves chopped, to garnish
1 small handful fresh dill, chopped,
   to garnish

The earthy sweetness of beetroot (beet) makes an excellent companion to rich walnuts in this vibrant salad. Garnished with fresh coriander (cilantro), this vivid dish is a feast for the eyes as well as the taste buds. (Pictured, right on page 16.)

If you are using fresh beetroot (beets), preheat the oven to 200°C/400°F/gas mark 6 and bake the beetroot for 1–1½ hours, until tender. Set aside to cool, then peel and coarsely grate or finely chop and set aside.

If using ready-cooked beetroot, coarsely grate or finely chop and set aside.

Place the walnuts in a food processor and process to a very fine paste. The paste should be sticky and smooth, but not at all grainy (this can take up to 5 minutes).

Crush the garlic with the back of a knife and then put in a mortar with a pinch of sea salt. Grind with a pestle to a smooth paste.

Place the walnut and garlic pastes in a bowl with the ground coriander, marigold, chilli powder and vinegar. Using your hands, bring the mixture together to a smooth, thick paste. The paste should be a similar texture to a loose hummus, so add a few drops of water if it is too thick.

Pour the walnut paste over the beetroot, then use your hands to bring everything together until well combined.

Place the mixture on a serving platter and garnish with fresh coriander (cilantro) and dill to serve. This can also be made ahead and refrigerated until ready to serve.

Khakhvis Pkhali

-SHALLOT PÂTÉ-

Preparation time: 10 minutes
Cooking time: 20 minutes
Serves 4–6 as part of a *supra*

1 kg/2 lb 3 oz banana shallots
200 g/7 oz/scant 1¾ cups chopped
    walnuts
1 tbsp apple cider vinegar or white
    wine vinegar
4 garlic cloves, crushed
1 handful fresh coriander (cilantro),
    leaves chopped, plus extra, to
    garnish
1 tsp dried coriander
1 green bird's eye chilli, finely
    chopped, or 1 tbsp *Mtsvane Ajika*
    (Green Chilli Paste, see page 31)
sea salt, to taste
1 tbsp chopped fresh dill, to garnish

Roasted in their skins, the shallots in this dish become deliciously soft and
sweet, making them the perfect foil for subtly spiced walnut paste. Fresh chilli
is added for a fiery kick (which I love), but you could leave this out if you prefer
a more delicate flavour. (Pictured, top-left on page 17.)

Preheat the oven to 200°C/400°F/gas mark 6.

Place the whole shallots, skin-on, on a large baking sheet and transfer to the
preheated oven to cook for 20 minutes, until soft with dry, papery skins. Set
aside to cool slightly.

While the shallots are cooking, place the fresh and dried coriander (cilantro),
garlic and chilli into a blender and blend to a smooth paste. Place in a small
bowl and set aside.

Place the walnuts in a food processor and process to a very fine paste. The
paste should be sticky and smooth, but not at all grainy (this can take up to
5 minutes).

Place the walnut paste in a bowl with the vinegar. Using your hands, bring
the mixture together to a smooth, thick paste. The paste should be a similar
texture to a loose hummus, so add a few drops of water if it is too thick. Pour
this mixture into the bowl with the coriander, garlic and chilli paste and stir to
combine.

Once the shallots are cool enough to handle, slice off their tops and squeeze out
their insides. Roughly chop the cooked shallots and transfer to the bowl with the
walnut and coriander mixture. Using your hands, combine everything together.
Season to taste and add more vinegar if necessary.

Place the mixture on a serving platter and spread out over the surface with the
back of a spoon. Scatter over fresh coriander and dill and serve. This can also be
made ahead and refrigerated until ready to serve.

Stapilos Pkhali

-CARROT PÂTÉ-

Preparation time: 10 minutes
Cooking time: 15 minutes
Serves 4–6 as part of a *supra*

1 kg/2 lb 3 oz carrots, peeled and left
    whole
200 g/7 oz/scant 1¾ cups chopped
    walnuts
3 garlic cloves
1 tsp ground coriander
1 tbsp apple cider vinegar or white
    wine vinegar
1 handful fresh coriander (cilantro),
    leaves chopped, to garnish
sea salt and chilli powder, to taste

When making this dish, you may find it unusual that the carrots are boiled whole and then diced into small cubes after cooking. The reason for this is that the small cubes of carrot are very easy to overcook and the success of this dish relies on them being just tender, but still retaining some of their crunch. (**Pictured, bottom-left on page 17.**)

Bring a large pan of water to a simmer over a medium heat, add the peeled carrots and cook until just tender, 10–15 minutes. Drain and leave to cool slightly, then dice into small cubes and set aside in a large bowl.

Place the walnuts in a food processor and process to a very fine paste. The paste should be sticky and smooth, but not at all grainy (this can take up to 5 minutes).

Crush the garlic with the back of a knife and then put in a mortar with a pinch each of sea salt and chilli powder. Grind with a pestle to a smooth paste.

Place the walnut and garlic pastes in a bowl with the ground coriander and vinegar. Using your hands, bring the mixture together to a smooth, thick paste. The paste should be a similar texture to a loose hummus, so add a few drops of water if it is too thick.

Add the walnut paste to the bowl with the carrots and use your hands to combine, ensuring that the carrots are well coated in the paste. Place the mixture on a serving platter and scatter over fresh coriander (cilantro) leaves to serve. This can also be made ahead and refrigerated until ready to serve.

Mtsvane Lobios Pkhali
-GREEN BEAN PÂTÉ-

Preparation time: 15 minutes
Cooking time: 25 minutes
Serves 4–6 as part of a *supra*

1 kg/2 lb 3 oz green beans, sliced
200 g/7 oz/scant 1¾ cups chopped
    walnuts
2 garlic cloves
3 tbsp vegetable oil
3 onions, finely chopped
1 tsp ground coriander
1 tsp dried ground marigold
1 tsp ground blue fenugreek
2 tbsp apple cider vinegar or white
    wine vinegar
1 bunch fresh parsley, leaves chopped
1 bunch fresh coriander (cilantro),
    leaves chopped
1 bunch fresh dill, chopped
sea salt and chilli powder, to taste

Despite the richness of the spiced walnut paste used to bind this recipe, the bite of the just-tender green beans and the fragrant aroma of the fresh herbs give it a light and summery flavour. This would make an excellent addition to a summer *supra*, eaten alfresco in the just-fading light of the evening sun. (Pictured, right on page 17.)

Place the green beans in a large pan and cover with boiling water. Place over a medium heat and bring to a simmer. Cook until just tender, around 8 minutes. Drain the beans through a colander and set aside to cool slightly. Once cool enough to handle, squeeze the beans with your hands to remove any excess water. Set aside.

Place the walnuts in a food processor and process to a very fine paste. The paste should be sticky and smooth, but not at all grainy (this can take up to 5 minutes).

Crush the garlic with the back of a knife and then put in a mortar with a pinch each of sea salt and chilli powder. Grind with a pestle to a smooth paste.

Heat the oil in a large frying pan (skillet) over a medium heat. Once hot, add the onions and cook, stirring continuously, until soft and just turning golden, about 15 minutes. Remove from the heat and set aside.

Place the walnut and garlic pastes in a bowl with the ground coriander, marigold, fenugreek and vinegar. Using your hands, bring the mixture together to a smooth, thick paste. The paste should be a similar texture to a loose hummus, so add a few drops of water if it is too thick.

Add the onions and beans to the walnut paste and stir to ensure everything is well coated in the sauce. Add the fresh herbs to the bowl and stir through again. Season to taste and serve.

Tkemali

-PLUM SAUCE-

Preparation time: 15 minutes
Cooking time: 35 minutes
Makes 1 large jar

2 kg/4 lb 6 ½ oz ripe plums
2 Bramley apples, peeled and grated
12 garlic cloves, crushed
1 handful fresh coriander (cilantro),
    roughly chopped
1 handful fresh dill, roughly chopped
1 fresh chilli, roughly chopped
pinch of sugar (optional)
pinch of lemon salt (optional)
sea salt and chilli powder, to taste

In Georgia, we start making this sauce as soon as the first plums began to ripen on the trees. Over the season, the flavour of the plums change and develop, from slightly sour to very sweet, so you could tell what time of the year it was just by tasting this sauce. It is delicious drizzled over meat or fish.

Slice a cross in the top of each plum, then place in a large, heavy based pan with 100 ml/3 ½ fl oz of water. Bring to a simmer, then leave to cook until the plums have started to break down and their skins have split. Pour the plums into a sieve (strainer) set over a large bowl and leave until cool enough to handle.

Once cooled, use a wooden spoon to press the flesh and juices of the plums through the sieve into the bowl below. Discard the skins and stones that are left in the sieve.

Return the plum mixture to the pan along with the grated apples and place over a low heat. Cook for around 10 minutes, until the apple has softened and broken down.

Meanwhile, place the garlic, herbs and chilli in a food processor and pulse until smooth. Add this mixture to the pan with the plums and continue to cook, stirring occasionally, for another 10 minutes. Season to taste with sea salt and chilli powder, then remove from the heat.

At this point, if the sauce is too sour, add a pinch of sugar; if it is too sweet, add a pinch of lemon salt. This can be served straight away, or stored in a large sterilized jar for up to 1 week in the fridge.

Tkemali

Plum sauce in Spring time

Unlike today, I never ate food that wasn't in season, and spring was the time when my favourite ingredients reappeared in the kitchen. All around there was the aroma of new potatoes, cucumber and *tkemali* (plum sauce). Spring heralded the start of the plum season and different varieties were used for plum sauce and bottled for the winter. This time of year would also mark the arrival of pink basil, which was my grandmother's favourite, and from which she would make a shocking pink basil syrup to add to tea, water and even vodka!

Brozeylis Satsebeli
-POMEGRANATE SAUCE-

Preparation time: 15 minutes
Cooking time: N/A
Serves 6–8

100 g/3 ½ oz/ ¾ cup walnut halves
2 garlic cloves
5 fresh coriander (cilantro) sprigs,
    leaves picked
500 ml/17 ½ fl oz/2 cups fresh
    pomegranate juice
120 ml/4 fl oz/ ½ cup distilled water
sea salt, to taste

Pomegranate seeds are vibrantly sweet with a sour end note that makes them the perfect base for this punchy sauce.

Place the walnuts in a food processor and process to a very fine paste. The paste should be sticky and smooth, but not at all grainy (this can take up to 5 minutes).

Crush the garlic with the back of a knife and then put in a mortar with the coriander (cilantro) leaves and a pinch of sea salt. Grind with a pestle to a smooth paste. Place the walnut and garlic pastes in a large bowl and mix to combine.

Place the pomegranate juice and water in a jug (pitcher) and whisk to combine. Gradually pour this liquid over the walnut and garlic paste, using your hands to dissolve the paste in the liquid as you do. Once the liquid is fully combined, season the sauce to taste with sea salt.

Mshrali Ajika

-DRY RED CHILLI PASTE-

Preparation time: 10 minutes
Cooking time: N/A
Makes 1 small pot

8 garlic cloves
2 tsp coarse sea salt
4 tsp dried chilli flakes
4 tsp ground coriander
2 tsp ground marigold
4 tsp ground blue fenugreek
2 tsp garlic powder

My grandmother used to call *ajika* a 'life saver' because it could bring any dish to life. It is very spicy, so do be warned that a little goes a long way. Of the three types of *ajika* in this book (see overleaf), this is the one to make if you will only be using a little at any one time because it is made mainly with dried ingredients and keeps for longer.

Crush the garlic with the back of a knife and then put in a mortar with a pinch of the sea salt. Grind with a pestle to a smooth paste and set aside.

Put the rest of the ingredients in a clean mortar and grind together with a pestle until fine and well combined. Add the garlic along with ½ tablespoon of water and mix to combine. This will keep in the fridge for up to 1 month.

Ziteli Ajika

-RED CHILLI PASTE-

Preparation time: 10 minutes
Cooking time: N/A
Makes 1 small pot

70 g/2 ½ oz red bird's eye chillies,
  roughly chopped
70 g/2 ½ oz long red peppers, deseeded
  and roughly chopped
30 g/1 oz fresh parsley, roughly
  chopped
30 g/1 oz fresh coriander (cilantro),
  roughly chopped
15 g/½ oz fresh basil leaves
15 g/½ oz celery leaves
15 g/½ oz garlic cloves, crushed
1 tsp ground blue fenugreek
1 tsp ground coriander
2 tsp sea salt
1 tsp ground marigold

No Georgian dinner table is complete without a pot of *ajika* for guests to pass round and spice their dishes with. This version, made with fresh red chillies and peppers, has the most complex flavour because behind the heat is an undertone of more mellow spice in the form of coriander, fenugreek and marigold.

Place the chillies, peppers, parsley, coriander (cilantro), basil, celery leaves and garlic into a food processor and process to a smooth, wet paste. Add the spices and stir through the paste to combine. This will keep in the fridge for 1 week.

Mtsvane Ajika

-GREEN CHILLI PASTE-

Preparation time: 10 minutes
Cooking time: N/A
Makes 1 small pot

200 g/7 oz green bird's eye chillies,
    roughly chopped
50 g/1¾ oz fresh coriander (cilantro),
    roughly chopped
50 g/1¾ oz fresh parsley, roughly
    chopped
50 g/1¾ oz fresh dill, roughly chopped
1 head of garlic, cloves crushed
1 tsp ground coriander
1 tbsp sea salt

My family love spice and my mother's favourite pick-me-up is a steaming cup of hot water infused with fresh green chilli. Despite our ingrained belief that red means danger, often green chillies are hotter than their more brightly hued counterparts. This is true in this case, and this is the spiciest of the three *ajika* recipes in this book, so use with moderation.

Put all of the ingredients except the ground coriander and salt in a food processor and process to a smooth, wet paste. Add the dried coriander and salt and stir through the paste to combine. This will keep in the fridge for 1 week.

Chutney

-GEORGIAN CHUTNEY-

Preparation time: 20 minutes
Cooking time: 30 minutes
Makes 1 large jar

6–7 tomatoes
zest of 1 lemon
1 onion, finely chopped
thumb-size piece of root ginger,
    peeled and grated
½ tsp dried ground marigold
½ tsp ground coriander
½ tsp ground blue fenugreek
sea salt and freshly ground black
    pepper

This smooth chutney made with tomatoes, ginger and spices can be made in bulk and frozen until needed. Excellent with cheese or cold meat, this can transform a simple supper into something special.

Preheat the oven to 200°C/400°F/gas mark 6.

Place the tomatoes on a baking sheet and transfer to the preheated oven to cook for 15–20 minutes, until soft.

Remove the tomatoes from the oven and carefully remove and discard the skins. Roughly chop the tomatoes and transfer the pulp and juices to a large pan with the lemon zest. Place over a medium heat and cook for 10 minutes, stirring continuously. Add the onion and ginger to the pan and continue to cook, stirring, for another 10 minutes.

Once cooked, transfer the tomato mixture to a blender with the spices. Blend until smooth and pour the mixture into a large sterilized jar. Once cooled, seal the jar and keep in the fridge for up to 1 week.

Salads

-CHAPTER 2-

Lobio

Beans, a Georgian staple

The 1990s was a very difficult time in Georgia. It was a period of great unrest and civil war, which resulted in Georgia losing Abkhazia, a beautiful region situated on the coast of the Black Sea. My family had a beautiful holiday home there, where we spent every summer and enjoyed so many happy memories, but suddenly all Georgians were expelled from the region. During this time, Russia cut off all supplies to Georgia and we suddenly found ourselves living with no electricity, water or gas for most of the time. It felt like a return to the Stone Age, but we had to rally round and find new ways of living so that we could survive. We learned to cook on oil burners, and neighbours would gather in each other's kitchens to learn these new skills and share their own. The shops were empty and basic goods were rationed. Families would start lining up for their ration of bread at 3–4 a.m. and the queues (lines) would snake their way round the streets, with people setting small fires to keep warm. Neighbours would take turns in the queues and despite all of the hardship, this was a time of great unity.

My grandmother, who had fled from the house in Abkhazia to find refuge with us, would spend her days coming up with new and inventive ways of using the beans or *lobio* to keep us well nourished, but also trying to keep our appetites stimulated when we had to eat the same food day in and day out. Because of the stress of losing her home, my grandmother became very ill and developed Parkinson's disease, but no matter how diminished she seemed, she was always her old self in the kitchen. For a few hours every day, food and its preparation seemed to bring her back to life.

Nigvziani Badrijani

-AUBERGINES STUFFED WITH WALNUT PASTE-

Preparation time: 20 minutes
Cooking time: 10 minutes
Serves 4–6 as part of a *supra*

2 medium aubergines (eggplant) cut
    lengthways into 5-mm/¼-inch slices
1 tbsp plus 1 tsp vegetable or
    sunflower oil
100 g/3½ oz spring onions (scallions),
    white parts only, finely sliced
100 g/3½ oz/scant 1 cup chopped
    walnuts
2 garlic cloves, crushed
½ tsp sea salt flakes
pinch of chilli flakes, or to taste
½ tsp ground marigold
½ tsp ground coriander
1 tsp ground blue fenugreek
1 tbsp apple cider vinegar or white
    wine vinegar
1 large handful fresh coriander
    (cilantro) leaves, chopped
1 small handful fresh parsley leaves,
    chopped
pomegranate seeds, to garnish

These delicate rolls of aubergine (eggplant) look and taste beautiful as part of a large table of sharing starters (appetizers) at a *supra*, especially when scattered with jewel-like pomegranate seeds. You can make these a day in advance, which makes them a great option if you are preparing lots of other dishes, because they can be whipped out of the fridge and onto the table at the last moment.

Preheat the oven to 200°C/400°F/gas mark 6 and line a large baking sheet with parchment paper.

Lay the aubergine (eggplant) slices on the prepared baking sheet and brush with 1 tablespoon of the vegetable or sunflower oil. Transfer to the preheated oven and cook until soft, around 5–10 minutes, turning halfway through. Place the cooked aubergine around the edges of a colander and set aside to cool and drain.

Heat the remaining oil in a frying pan (skillet) over a medium heat, then add the sliced spring onions (scallions) and cook until soft. Transfer to a bowl and set aside to cool.

Place the walnuts in a food processor and process on a high speed until you have a smooth, wet paste. Transfer the walnut paste to a small bowl and set aside.

Put the crushed garlic cloves, salt and chilli flakes in a mortar and grind with a pestle until the mixture has a very smooth consistency. Add the garlic mixture to the walnut paste along with the marigold, ground coriander, fenugreek and vinegar, then use your hands to dissolve the walnut and garlic pastes in the vinegar. Add the cooled spring onions, half of the fresh coriander (cilantro) and all of the parsley and mix thoroughly to combine into a thick paste.

Working one at a time, take an aubergine slice and spread one side with a generous spoonful of the walnut paste, roll the slice lengthways to encase the filling and then spread an additional teaspoon of the walnut paste on top of the piece of rolled aubergine. Transfer to a serving plate and repeat with the remaining aubergine slices. Serve, garnished with pomegranate seeds and the remaining fresh coriander.

Ziteli Lobios Salata

-WINTER KIDNEY BEAN SALAD-

Preparation time: 15 minutes
Cooking time: 40 minutes
Serves 4–6 as part of a *supra*

4 x 400-g/14-oz cans kidney beans
100 ml/3 ½ fl oz/scant ½ cup vegetable
  or sunflower oil
4 onions, cut in half, then finely sliced
1 ½ tsp ground cinnamon
2 tsp ground coriander
½ tsp hot chilli powder, or to taste
2 tbsp apple cider vinegar or white
  wine vinegar
sea salt and chilli powder, to taste
1 handful fresh coriander (cilantro),
  leaves chopped, to garnish

This bean salad is spiced with the warming flavours of coriander and cinnamon, making it perfect for serving during the colder months. This recipe uses canned beans, meaning that it can be put together relatively quickly without factoring in any time for soaking.

Place a large sieve (strainer) or colander over a bowl and drain the kidney beans through it, reserving the drained liquid. Set aside.

Place the oil in a large pan over a medium heat. Once hot, add the onions and cook, stirring continuously, until soft and just starting to turn golden, about 10 minutes. Add the drained kidney beans to the pan and stir to combine, reduce the heat to low and continue to cook, covered, but stirring occasionally, for 15–20 minutes. If the mixture starts to looks too dry, add a little of the reserved kidney bean water to the pan.

Remove the lid from the pan and add the cinnamon, ground coriander and chilli powder and stir to combine. Continue to cook, uncovered and stirring occasionally, for another 10 minutes, adding more of the reserved liquid if necessary. Remove from the heat and set aside to cool to room temperature.

Once the mixture has cooled, stir through the vinegar and season to taste with sea salt and chilli powder. Transfer the salad to a serving platter, garnish with fresh coriander (cilantro) and serve cold. This can also be made ahead and refrigerated until ready to serve.

Kirkaji

-SUMMER KIDNEY BEAN SALAD-

Preparation time: 10 minutes
Cooking time: N/A
Serves 4–6 as part of a *supra*

3 x 400-g/14-oz cans kidney beans
3 onions, halved and finely sliced
1 spring onion (scallion), green part
  only, finely sliced
1 small bunch fresh parsley, leaves
  chopped
1 large bunch fresh coriander
  (cilantro), leaves chopped
1 small bunch fresh tarragon, leaves
  chopped (optional)
150 ml/5 fl oz/generous ½ cup
  vegetable or sunflower oil
4 tbsp apple cider vinegar or white
  wine vinegar
1 fresh green chilli, finely chopped, or
  to taste (optional)
sea salt and chilli powder, to taste

This variation of a classic Georgian bean salad is packed with fragrant fresh herbs for a more summery feel. These salads are eaten throughout the year and supplemented with the best produce available as the seasons roll by.

Place a large sieve (strainer) or colander over a bowl and drain the kidney beans through it, ensuring that you reserve the drained liquid. Place the beans in a large mixing bowl and add the remaining ingredients, mixing until everything is well distributed. Season to taste with sea salt and add more fresh green chilli or chilli powder if you like. If the mixture seems too dry, add a couple of spoonfuls of the reserved liquid from the kidney beans.

This can be served immediately or made up to a day ahead and refrigerated until just before serving.

Nigvziani Ziteli Lobio
-KIDNEY BEAN SALAD WITH WALNUTS-

Preparation time: 15 minutes
Cooking time: 10 minutes
Serves 4–6 as part of a *supra*

3 tbsp vegetable or sunflower oil
3 onions, halved and finely sliced
200 g/7 oz/scant 1¾ cups chopped
   walnuts
2 tsp ground coriander
1 tsp ground marigold
1 tsp ground cinnamon
½ tsp ground cloves
2 tbsp apple cider vinegar or white
   wine vinegar
3 x 400-g/14-oz cans kidney beans,
   drained
1 large bunch fresh coriander
   (cilantro), leaves chopped or seeds
   from 1 pomegranate, to garnish
sea salt and chilli powder, to taste

This bean salad is given added richness and depth of flavour by the addition of a spiced walnut paste base. These ingredients would have been cheap and readily available in times when fresh meat and vegetables were hard to come by, but it still succeeds in feeling rich and celebratory even now.

Place the oil in a large pan over a medium heat. Once hot, add onions and cook, stirring continuously, until soft and translucent, about 10 minutes.

Meanwhile, place the walnuts in a food processor and process to a very fine paste. The paste should be sticky and smooth, but not at all grainy (this can take up to 5 minutes).

Place the walnut paste in a bowl with the ground coriander, ground marigold, ground cinnamon, ground cloves and vinegar. Using your hands bring the mixture together to a smooth, thick paste. The paste should be a similar texture to a loose hummus, so add a few drops of water if it is too thick.

Place the beans in a large mixing bowl with the onions and stir until well combined. Add the spiced walnut paste to the bowl and stir again until everything is well coated in the paste. Season to taste with sea salt and chilli powder. This can be served straight away or refrigerated until needed. Garnish with fresh coriander (cilantro) or pomegranate seeds just before serving.

Nigvziani Katmis Salata

-CHICKEN SALAD WITH WALNUTS-

Preparation time: 15 minutes
Cooking time: 45 minutes
Serves 4–6 as part of a *supra*

1 kg/2 lb 3 oz chicken breasts
3 tbsp vegetable or sunflower oil
3 onions, finely chopped
200 g/7 oz/scant 1¾ cups chopped walnuts
1 large bunch fresh dill, leaves chopped
1 tsp ground coriander
1 tsp dried ground marigold
4 garlic cloves
1½ tbsp mayonnaise
sea salt and chilli powder, to taste

Although this is a salad, it is quite rich, and a little goes a long way. If you are lucky enough to have leftovers, try it spread over fresh bread for lunch or a mid-morning snack.

Bring a large pan of water to the boil over a medium heat and add the chicken breasts. Bring the water back to the boil, then reduce the heat to a simmer and cook, covered, for 30 minutes. Use a knife to check that the chicken is cooked through, then drain and set aside until cool enough to handle.

Heat the oil in a large frying pan (skillet) over a medium heat. Once hot add the onions and cook, stirring continuously, until soft and just turning golden, about 15 minutes. Set aside to cool.

Meanwhile, place the walnuts in a food processor and process to a very fine paste. The paste should be sticky and smooth, but not at all grainy (this can take up to 5 minutes).

Once the chicken has cooled, use your hands to shred the flesh, then add it to a large bowl along with the onions.

Add the walnut paste, dill, spices, garlic and mayonnaise to the bowl and mix everything until well combined. Season to taste with sea salt and chilli powder and serve.

Shavi Lobios Salata

-BLACK BEAN SALAD-

Preparation time: 10 minutes
Cooking time: 25 minutes
Serves 4–6 as part of a *supra*

100 ml/3 ½ fl oz sunflower or vegetable
   oil
3 onions, halved and finely sliced
2 tsp ground coriander
4 tsp summer savoury
1 kg/2 lb 3 oz canned black beans,
   drained and liquid reserved
5 garlic cloves
1 bunch fresh coriander (cilantro),
   leaves chopped, to garnish
sea salt and chilli powder, to taste

Black beans are rich and have a dense, meaty texture that makes them ideal for using in vegetarian salads. You can buy dried versions, but for speed I have used the canned kind here. If you want to, add long red peppers to bring a sweet undertone and lift the punch of the almost-raw garlic. This can be served hot straight from the pan after cooking or left to cool and served at room temperature.

Heat the oil in a large frying pan (skillet) over a medium heat. Once hot, add the onions and cook, stirring continuously, until soft but not coloured, about 10 minutes. Add the ground coriander and summer savoury and cook, stirring, for 2 minutes more.

Add the beans to the pan and stir to coat in the onions and spices. Reduce the heat to low and cook, covered but stirring occasionally, for 10–15 minutes.

Meanwhile, crush the garlic with the back of a knife and then put in a mortar with a pinch of sea salt. Grind with a pestle to a smooth paste.

Remove the lid from the pan and add the garlic. Cook, stirring for a final 3 minutes, then remove from the heat, season to taste with sea salt and chilli powder and transfer to a serving bowl.

If you are serving the dish hot, garnish with the coriander (cilantro) and serve immediately. If you are serving cooled, allow the beans to cool to room temperature before garnishing with the coriander.

Badrijnis Salata

-AUBERGINE SALAD-

Preparation time: 10 minutes
Cooking time: 40 minutes
Serves 4–6 as part of a *supra*

1 kg/2 lb 3 oz aubergines (eggplants),
    approximately 3 medium aubergines
2 tbsp vegetable or sunflower oil
2 onions, halved and finely sliced
1 tsp dried basil
200 g/7 oz/scant 1¾ cups chopped
    walnuts
3 garlic cloves
1 tsp ground coriander
1 tsp ground marigold
½ tsp hot chilli powder, or to taste
1 handful fresh coriander (cilantro),
    leaves chopped or seeds from
    1 pomegranate, to garnish
sea salt and chilli powder, to taste

Growing up in Georgia, aubergines (eggplant) were only available at certain times of the year, but we looked forward to their arrival with great anticipation. Nowadays (both in Georgia and here in the UK) they are available year-round, but their flavour doesn't match those I remember from my youth. One consolation for this is that I no longer have to wait to make classic dishes featuring aubergines.

Preheat the oven to 200°C/400°F/gas mark 6.

Slice the aubergine (eggplant) lengthways into 1-cm/½-inch slices, lay on a baking sheet and brush on both sides with half of the oil. Transfer to the preheated oven and cook for 20 minutes, turning halfway through, until soft and golden. Lay the slices over the edges of a colander and set aside to drain.

Place the remaining oil in a frying pan (skillet) over a medium heat. Once hot, gently fry the onions, stirring continuously, until soft and just starting to turn golden, around 10 minutes. Stir the dried basil through the onions and set aside.

Slice the dark skin from the edges of the cooled aubergine slices and discard. Roughly chop the aubergine flesh and add to the pan with the onions. Return the pan to the heat and cook for 3–4 minutes, stirring continuously.

Place a sieve (strainer) over a bowl and tip in the onion and aubergine mixture. Set aside to drain for 15 minutes, being careful not to dispose of any of the drained liquid.

Put the walnuts in a food processor and process to a very fine paste. The paste should be sticky and smooth, but not at all grainy (this can take up to 5 minutes).

Crush the garlic with the back of a knife and then put in a mortar with a pinch each of sea salt and chilli powder. Grind with a pestle to a smooth paste.

Place the walnut and garlic pastes in a bowl with the ground coriander, marigold and chilli powder. Using your hands, bring the mixture together to a smooth, thick paste.

Place the drained aubergine and onion mixture in a large bowl and add the walnut paste. Use your hands to mix everything together, adding some of the water drained from the aubergines and onions if the mixture is too thick.

Place the mixture on a serving platter and spread out over the surface with the back of a spoon. Scatter over fresh coriander (cilantro) or pomegranate seeds and serve. This can also be made ahead and refrigerated until ready to serve.

Mtsvane Lobios Salata

-GREEN BEAN AND RED PEPPER SALAD-

Preparation time: 10 minutes
Cooking time: 30 minutes
Serves 4–6 as part of a *supra*

1 kg/2 lb 3 oz green beans, sliced
5 garlic cloves
150 ml/5 fl oz/generous ½ cup
    vegetable or sunflower oil
3–4 onions, finely chopped
1 large carrot, peeled and coarsely
    grated
2 long red peppers, finely sliced
1 tbsp tomato purée (paste)
2 tsp demerara (turbinado) sugar
50 g/1¾ oz fresh parsley, chopped
50 g/1¾ oz fresh dill, chopped
50 g/1¾ oz fresh coriander (cilantro),
    chopped
sea salt and hot chilli powder, to taste

This salad makes a deliciously fresh way to start a meal, but would also work well as a side dish alongside simple grilled meat or fish. The beans are lightly cooked to retain some bite and paired with a fragrant medley of fresh herbs making this the perfect addition to any spring or summer dining table.

Bring a large pan of water to the boil then add the beans. Lower the heat to a gentle simmer and cook for 4 minutes, or until just tender. Drain and rinse in cold water to stop cooking. Using your hands, pick up the beans and squeeze them to remove any excess water. Set aside.

Crush the garlic with the back of a knife and then put in a mortar with a pinch of sea salt. Grind with a pestle to a smooth paste and set aside.

Heat the oil in large sauté pan over a medium heat. Add the onions to the pan and cook, stirring continuously, until soft and starting to turn golden, about 10 minutes. Add the grated carrot and continue to cook, stirring, until softened but still retaining some bite. Add the peppers to the pan and cook for another 3 minutes.

Using a wooden spoon or spatula, push the vegetables to the side of the pan. Add the tomato purée (paste) and demerara (turbinado) sugar to the centre of the pan and cook, stirring, for around 2 minutes, until thickened. Combine the vegetables in the pan with the tomato purée (paste), then add the beans to the pan and stir to combine. Cook for 5–7 minutes, stirring occasionally. Add the garlic paste, chilli powder and fresh herbs to the pan and cook for a final 2 minutes.

Transfer to a serving platter and serve warm.

Ziteli Bulgaruli Zizakis Salata

-RED PEPPER AND WALNUT SALAD-

Preparation time: 10 minutes
Cooking time: 10 minutes
Serves 4–6 as part of a *supra*

90 g/5 ½ oz/1 cup walnut halves
150 ml/5 fl oz/generous ½ cup
  vegetable or sunflower oil
5 tbsp apple cider vinegar or white
  wine vinegar
1 tsp caster (superfine) sugar
½ tsp salt
500 g/1 lb 2 oz sweet pointed red
  peppers, deseeded and sliced into
  2.5-cm/1-inch chunks
2 tsp *Mtsvane Ajika* (Green Chilli
  Paste, see page 31)
50 g/3 ½ oz fresh coriander (cilantro)
  leaves, chopped

Although it looks simple, this dish is all about balance: deliciously sweet red peppers are contrasted with rich walnut paste and the *Ajika* adds a hit of chilli heat. The poaching liquid that the peppers are cooked in can be stored in the fridge and reused another time.

Place the walnuts in a food processor and process to a very fine paste. The paste should be sticky and smooth, but not at all grainy (this can take up to 5 minutes). Set aside.

Place the oil, vinegar, sugar and salt in a small pan over a medium heat and bring to the boil. Once boiling, reduce the heat to a simmer and add the pepper to the pan. Cover the pan and cook for 7–8 minutes, until the peppers are tender but not falling apart.

Drain the peppers, reserving the sauce to be used another time. Place the peppers in a bowl with the walnut paste and *Ajika* and use your hands to bring the mixture together and coat the peppers in the walnut paste. Add 1 tablespoon of water if the mixture is too dry.

Garnish with fresh coriander (cilantro) and serve.

Akhali Kartophili

-NEW POTATOES WITH CHILLI AND HERBS-

Preparation time: 10 minutes
Cooking time: 25 minutes
Serves 6

1 kg/2 lb 3 oz new potatoes
50 g/1¾ oz butter
2 tbsp vegetable or sunflower oil
1 green chilli, finely chopped
1 bunch spring onions (scallions),
    finely sliced
3 garlic cloves, crushed
25 g/1 oz fresh dill, chopped
25 g/1 oz fresh coriander (cilantro),
    chopped
sea salt and freshly ground black
    pepper

These potatoes, spiced with fiery chilli and fragrant with fresh herbs, would make an excellent accompaniment to any of the stews in the main course section of this book. Both soft and crunchy, they are boiled until tender and then fried until just crispy and golden on the outside.

Place the potatoes in a large pan with 2.5 cm/1 inch of water. Place over a medium heat and bring just to the boil. Reduce the heat to a simmer and cook, covered, for 15 minutes, until tender. Drain.

In a separate pan, heat the butter and oil over a medium heat. Once hot, add the chilli, spring onions (scallions) and garlic and fry, stirring continuously, until soft and just turning golden.

Add the potatoes to the pan and shake to coat. Continue to cook them, stirring occasionally, until the potatoes are just turning golden. Add the herbs to the pan and stir through. Season to taste and serve.

Sokos Pkhali Nigvizit

-MUSHROOM SALAD WITH WALNUTS-

Preparation time: 15 minutes
Cooking time: 20 minutes
Serves 4–6 as part of a *supra*

3 tbsp vegetable or sunflower oil
4 onions, finely chopped
1 kg/2 lb 3 oz button mushrooms,
    stalks removed and finely diced
200 g/7 oz/scant 1¾ cups chopped
    walnuts
1 tsp *Ajika* of your choice (Chilli
    Paste, see pages 28–31)
sea salt and freshly ground black
    pepper
1 handful fresh coriander (cilantro),
    leaves chopped, to garnish

When the warmer months are drawing to a close, the vibrant produce of summer makes way to more autumnal flavours. Mushrooms, when combined with the classic flavour of walnuts, make for an earthy and comforting salad.

Place the oil in a large pan over a medium heat. Once hot, add the onions and cook, stirring continuously, until soft and just starting to turn golden, about 10 minutes. Add the mushrooms to the pan and continue to cook, stirring, until all of the water released from the mushrooms has evaporated, about 10 minutes. Transfer the mixture to a large bowl and set aside to cool.

Place the walnuts in a food processor and process to a very fine paste. The paste should be sticky and smooth, but not at all grainy (this can take up to 5 minutes). Place the walnut paste in a bowl, stir through the *Ajika* and season to taste.

When the mushroom and onion mixture has cooled to room temperature, pour over the walnut and *Ajika* mixture and stir to combine, ensuring that the mushrooms are well coated in the walnut paste.

Place the mixture on a serving platter and scatter over fresh coriander (cilantro) to serve. This can also be made ahead and refrigerated until ready to serve.

Right: My grandmother at home in Georgia in 1951.

Soups

-CHAPTER 3-

Bebia's Supi
-GRANDMOTHER'S SOUP-

Preparation time: 25 minutes
Cooking time: 30 minutes
Serves 6

3 medium white potatoes, peeled and
    cut into bite-sized chunks
1 red (bell) pepper, sliced
2 carrots, peeled and sliced
2 bay leaves
4 black peppercorns
4 garlic cloves
4 shallots, peeled
3 fresh dill sprigs, chopped
3 fresh parsley sprigs, leaves chopped
2 tbsp vegetable or sunflower oil
30 g/1 oz butter
2 onions, finely chopped
2 x 400-g/14-oz cans chopped
    tomatoes
3 tbsp vermicelli pasta
1 tsp chilli powder, or to taste
sea salt, to taste

My maternal grandmother was very strict and had a lot of rules surrounding food. One of them was that soup had to be served at every meal, and nine times out of ten, this is the soup she served. When I was younger I didn't like this soup, possibly because I was forced to eat it so often, but these days I have grown much fonder of it and the memories it brings.

Place 3 litres/5¼ pints of boiling water in a large pan over a medium heat. Add the potatoes, red (bell) pepper, carrots, bay leaves, peppercorns, whole garlic cloves, whole shallots and herb sprigs to the pan and bring back to the boil, then reduce the heat to a simmer and leave to cook, uncovered, for 15 minutes.

Meanwhile, place the oil and butter in a pan over a medium heat. Once hot, add the onions and cook, stirring continuously, until soft but not coloured, about 10 minutes. Add the chopped tomatoes to the pan and stir to combine. Leave to cook for another 10 minutes, stirring occasionally.

Lift the herb sprigs out of the soup and discard. When the potatoes are almost tender, add the vermicelli to the pan and cook for 5 minutes, then add the tomato and onion mixture and stir to combine. Add the chilli powder to the soup and season to taste with sea salt. Transfer to serving bowls and serve hot.

Right: My grandmothers sharing a toast.

Bebia's Supi

Memories of my Grandmother's soup

My two grandmothers had very different approaches to food; for one it was a celebration, for the other a discipline. When it came to food, my maternal grandmother was very conventional and, because of this, I always dreaded visiting her home. When my family visited her, there was absolutely no eating between meals, which was in stark contrast to my paternal grandmother's house, where we were always raiding the fridge to devour the goodies that she kept there. Another rule that my maternal grandmother had, and one that was even harder for me to follow, was that every meal had to start with soup.

Without fail, at the start of every mealtime a large bowl of steaming soup was placed in front of me and, also without fail, I battled with my grandmother about not wanting to eat it. I wasn't allowed to leave the table or continue with my meal until at least some of the soup had been consumed, so eventually we would compromise and I would force down a few meagre mouthfuls to keep her happy. My grandmother tried everything to get me to eat her soup, from filling it with my favourite vegetables to buying me a special brightly patterned bowl to eat it from, but nothing ever did the trick. These days I love soup and eat it regularly, but I can never sit down to a bowl without a wry smile in remembrance of the battle of wills that my grandmother and I staged over the dinner table all those years ago.

Lobios Supi

-BEAN SOUP-

Preparation time: 10 minutes, plus at
    least 2 hours' soaking time
Cooking time: 1 hour 15 minutes
Serves 4–6

500 g/1 lb 2 oz dried beans (kidney,
    borlotti [cranberry] or cannellini
    beans or a mix), rinsed and soaked
    in cold water for at least 2 hours or
    up to overnight
2 litres/3 ½ pints cold water
3 tbsp vegetable or sunflower oil
3 onions, finely chopped
1 bay leaf
2 tsp *Mtsvane Ajika* (Green Chilli
    Paste, see page 31)
50 g/1 ¾ oz celery, finely chopped
1 small bunch fresh coriander
    (cilantro), leaves chopped
sea salt and freshly ground black
    pepper

This hearty soup is perfect for cold days when you are craving something warm,
comforting and filling with just a hint of chilli heat to awaken your senses. The
beans are mashed to give the soup a thick texture, which I enjoy, but liquid can
be added to achieve a thinner consistency if you prefer.

Drain the beans and place them in a large pan with enough of the water to
completely cover. Place over a medium heat and bring to a gentle simmer. Cook
for 40 minutes, until the beans are tender, gradually adding more of the water as
the beans swell and absorb the liquid. Drain the beans, reserving the liquid, and
return to the pan. Using a potato masher, mash the cooked beans until almost
smooth (I like to leave a few lumps for texture). Set aside in the pan.

Heat the oil in a large frying pan (skillet) over a medium heat. Once hot, add
the onions and cook, stirring continuously, until soft and just golden, about
10 minutes.

Add the cooked onions to the pan with the beans and enough of the reserved
water to achieve a consistency that you are happy with. I like my soup quite
thick, but this will depend on personal taste. Bring to a simmer, then add the bay
leaf and *Ajika* and continue to cook, stirring occasionally, for 10 minutes.

Remove the bay leaf from the pan and discard. Add the celery and coriander
(cilantro) to the pan and cook for another 4 minutes, stirring occasionally.
Season to taste and serve hot.

Tarkhunis Supi
-TARRAGON SOUP-

Preparation time: 45 minutes
Cooking time: 20 minutes
Serves 4–6

4 medium potatoes, peeled and cut
    into bite-sized chunks
50 g/1¾ oz butter
3 tbsp vegetable or sunflower oil
3 onions, finely chopped
4 garlic cloves, crushed
3 carrots, peeled and grated
1 large bunch fresh tarragon, leaves
    picked
3 mint sprigs, leaves chopped
3 eggs
½ tsp apple cider vinegar or white
    wine vinegar
sea salt and chilli powder, to taste

Tarragon is one of my favourite herbs and, along with dill, coriander (cilantro) and basil, is one of the most commonly used in Georgian cuisine. Its distinctive aniseed flavour has an almost metallic edge which can drown out subtler flavours. Because of this, I think it's best used in recipes where it is the main ingredient, such as this soup or the *Tarkhunis Perogi* (**Tarragon Pie**) on page 174.

Place the potatoes in a large pan with 1.5 litres/2¾ pints of cold water. Place over a high heat and bring to a boil, then reduce the heat to a simmer and leave to cook until tender, about 15 minutes.

Meanwhile, place the butter and oil in a large pan over a medium heat. Once the butter has melted, add the onions and garlic and cook, stirring continuously, until soft and just turning golden, about 15 minutes. Add the carrots to the pan and cook, stirring, for another 5 minutes, until just tender.

Once the potatoes are tender, drain through a colander, reserving the water. Add the potatoes to the pan with the onions and carrot mixture and stir to combine. Add the reserved water, bring to a simmer and cook for another 5 minutes.

Add the fresh herbs to the pan and stir to combine. Cook for 3 minutes and season to taste with sea salt and chilli powder. Remove the pan from the heat and leave to cool for 5 minutes.

Place the eggs in a small bowl with the vinegar and beat until smooth. Add the egg mixture to the pan and whisk to incorporate. Return the pan to the heat, bring back to a simmer and cook, stirring continuously, for a final 5 minutes. Check the seasoning and serve hot.

Borscht

-BEETROOT SOUP-

Preparation time: 15 minutes
Cooking time: 35 minutes
Serves 6

4 fresh beetroot (beets), peeled and
    coarsely grated
1 pinch lemon salt
150 ml/5 fl oz/generous ½ cup
    vegetable or sunflower oil
2 onions, finely chopped
1 small fennel bulb, finely chopped
1 tbsp tomato purée (paste)
2 tsp brown sugar
2 x 400-g/14-oz cans chopped
    tomatoes
2.5 litres/4½ pints water
2 Granny Smith apples, grated
4 garlic cloves, crushed
15 g/½ oz fresh parsley, chopped
30 g/1 oz fresh dill, chopped
crème fraîche or sour cream, to serve
sea salt and freshly ground black
    pepper

Although borscht is most commonly associated with Russian or Ukrainian cuisine, it has been adopted into Georgian culture. Borscht was one of the mainstays of my grandmother's table. She made hers with cabbage and I always had to force it down. Years later, when making my own version I steered clear of cabbage and added apple and fennel instead, which adds a delicious sweetness to the mellow beetroot (beet) flavour with a delicious tang of aniseed coming from the fresh fennel.

Place the beetroot (beets) in a bowl and sprinkle over the lemon salt. Set aside.

Heat the oil in a large pan over a medium heat. Once hot, add the onions and fennel and cook, stirring continuously, for 15 minutes, until soft and translucent. Using a wooden spoon or spatula, push the onions to the side of the pan. Add the tomato purée (paste) and sugar to the centre of the pan and cook, stirring, for around 2 minutes, until thickened, then add the chopped tomatoes and stir everything to combine.

Retain 1 tablespoon of the beetroot and add the rest to the pan. Cook, stirring occasionally, for 10 minutes, until the beetroot has started to soften, then add the water and bring to a simmer.

Squeeze the grated apple over the pan to release any juices, then add the grated flesh to the pan and stir to combine. Cook for 5 minutes more then stir in the garlic, remaining tablespoon of beetroot, parsley and half of the dill. Season to taste.

Divide the soup between serving bowls and garnish with the remaining dill and a spoonful of crème fraîche or sour cream. Serve hot.

Chikhirtma

-CHICKEN AND EGG SOUP-

Preparation time: 10 minutes
Cooking time: 1 hour
Serves 6

1 medium chicken (approximately
    1.8 kg/4 lb)
70 g/2½ oz butter
3 onions, chopped
1 large bunch fresh coriander
    (cilantro)
2 tbsp plain (all-purpose) flour
pinch of ground cinnamon (optional)
5 egg yolks
2 tbsp apple cider vinegar or white
    wine vinegar
sea salt and chilli powder, to taste

When making chicken dishes, such as this soup, I like to start with a whole chicken and boil it to make a really rich base broth. The carcass can be saved and cooked again for stock, making this economical as well as delicious. It's also a great hangover cure!

Place the chicken in a large pan with 1.5 litres/2¾ pints of cold water over a high heat. Bring just to the boil, then reduce the heat to a simmer and cook for 45 minutes, until the chicken is cooked through and tender.

Place a colander over a large bowl and strain the chicken, retaining the stock. Set the chicken and stock aside to cool.

Meanwhile, place the butter in a large pan over a medium heat. Once melted and bubbling, add the onions and cook, stirring continuously, until soft and just turning golden, about 15 minutes.

Add the retained stock to the pan and bring the mixture to a boil. Once boiling, reduce the heat to a simmer and add half of the coriander (cilantro) bunch, including the stems, to the pan and leave to cook for 10 minutes.

Meanwhile, place the flour in a small bowl with a few drops of cold water and mix to a thick paste. Add the flour paste to the pan along with a pinch of cinnamon (if using). Whisk the mixture to break up the flour and leave to simmer for another 20 minutes until the soup is slightly thickened.

Lift the coriander out of the pan and discard. Take the pan off the heat and set aside for 5 minutes to cool slightly.

Place the egg yolks in a small bowl with the vinegar and beat until smooth. Add the egg mixture to the pan and whisk to incorporate. Return the pan to the heat, bring back to a simmer and cook, stirring continuously, for a final 5 minutes. Season to taste with sea salt and chilli powder and remove from the heat.

Once the chicken is cool enough to handle, strip the flesh from the carcass and divide it between serving bowls. Ladle over the soup and serve, garnished with leaves from the remaining coriander.

Chikhirtma (Vegetarianuli)

-EGG AND CORIANDER SOUP-

Preparation time: 10 minutes
Cooking time: 1 hour
Serves 6

70 g/2½ oz butter
3 onions, chopped
1 large bunch fresh coriander
   (cilantro)
1 tbsp plain (all-purpose) flour
pinch of ground cinnamon (optional)
4 eggs
2 tsp apple cider vinegar or white wine
   vinegar
sea salt and freshly ground black
   pepper

This is the vegetarian version of the classic Georgian chicken and egg soup. The soup is unique in that it is thickened with eggs and contains almost no vegetable base. It is important that the soup is left off the heat for several minutes before the eggs are added, because otherwise they will scramble the moment that they touch the broth.

Place the butter in a large pan over a medium heat. Once melted and bubbling, add the onions and cook, stirring continuously, until soft and just turning golden, about 15 minutes.

Add 1.5 litres/2¾ pints of boiling water and half of the coriander (cilantro) bunch, including the stems, to the pan. Bring the mixture back to the boil, reduce to a simmer and leave to cook for 10 minutes.

Meanwhile, place the flour in a small bowl with a few drops of cold water and mix to a thick paste. Add the flour paste to the pan along with a pinch of cinnamon (if using). Whisk the mixture to break up the flour and leave to simmer for another 20 minutes until the soup is slightly thickened.

Lift the coriander out of the pan and discard. Take the pan off the heat and set aside for 5 minutes to cool slightly.

Place the eggs in a small bowl with the vinegar and beat until smooth. Add the egg mixture to the pan and whisk to incorporate. Return the pan to the heat, bring back to a simmer and cook, stirring continuously, for a final 5 minutes. Check the seasoning and serve hot, garnished with leaves from the remaining coriander.

Matzvnis

-SOUR CREAM SOUP-

Preparation time: 15 minutes
Cooking time: 40 minutes
Serves 6

50 g/1¾ oz butter
3 onions, finely chopped
1 carrot, peeled and grated
500 ml/18 fl oz/2¼ cups sour cream
500 ml/18 fl oz/2 cups whole milk
2 eggs
dash of apple cider vinegar or white
    wine vinegar
2 tbsp plain (all-purpose) flour
20 g/¾ oz fresh basil leaves, torn
20 g/¾ oz mint leaves, chopped
1 fresh green chilli, chopped, or to
    taste
sea salt and chilli powder, to taste

When I first served this dish at my Hackney-based café, customers shied away from it because they seemed to struggle with the idea of a soup flavoured with sour cream. Luckily, a few brave customers eventually gave it a go and now it is something I am asked for on a regular basis, even when it isn't on the menu!

Melt the butter in large pan over a medium heat. Once melted and bubbling, add the onions and cook, stirring continuously, until soft and translucent, about 10 minutes. Add the carrots to the pan and continue to cook, stirring, for another 5 minutes.

In a large bowl or jug (pitcher), combine the sour cream and milk and whisk together until well combined. Pour this mixture over the onions and stir to combine. Bring the mixture to a gentle simmer and leave to cook, stirring occasionally, for 10 minutes.

Meanwhile, beat the eggs with the vinegar in a small bowl. Add the flour and beat until well combined.

Remove the soup from the heat and leave to cool slightly for around 5 minutes. While stirring continuously, slowly pour the egg mixture into the soup until combined. Return the pan to the heat, bring to a simmer and cook, stirring occasionally, for 5 minutes.

Stir the fresh herbs into the soup and season to taste with sea salt and chilli powder. Divide the soup among bowls and serve with the fresh chilli so that everyone can spice the soup according to their own tastes.

Katmis Supi

-CHICKEN AND VEGETABLE SOUP-

Preparation time: 25 minutes
Cooking time: 1 hour 15 minutes
Serves 6

1 medium chicken (approximately
    1.8 kg/4 lb)
1 onion, finely chopped
3 medium white potatoes, cut into
    bite-sized chunks
2 carrots, peeled and finely diced
2 tbsp butter (optional)
4 black peppercorns
4 parsley sprigs (2 sprigs whole,
    2 sprigs chopped)
4 dill sprigs (2 sprigs whole, 2 sprigs
    chopped)
2 garlic cloves, crushed
10 g/¼ oz celery, finely chopped
sea salt and chilli powder, to taste

This chunky soup is filling, full of flavour and great for boosting the spirits. The garlic is added at the end of cooking to add a little pungent fire, which you could add to with a spoonful or two of *Ajika* (Chilli Paste, see pages 28–31) if you like.

Place the chicken in a large pan with 1.5 litres/2¾ pints/6 cups of cold water over a high heat. Bring just to the boil, then reduce the heat to a simmer and cook for 45 minutes, until the chicken is cooked through and tender.

Place a colander over a large bowl and strain the chicken, retaining the stock. Set the chicken aside to cool. Return the stock to the pan and bring back to a simmer. Add the onion, potatoes, carrots, butter (if using), peppercorns, whole parsley and dill sprigs and most of the garlic, and leave to cook until the potatoes are tender, about 20 minutes. Remove the herb sprigs from the pan and discard.

Once the chicken is cool enough to handle, strip the meat from the carcass and set aside.

Mix the remaining herbs and remaining garlic with the celery in a small bowl, then add to the pan and stir to combine. Now add the meat from the chicken and leave to cook for 5 minutes. Season to taste with sea salt and chilli powder and serve hot.

Soup Kharcho (Vegetarianuli)
-SPICED RICE AND TOMATO SOUP-

Preparation time: 10 minutes
Cooking time: 40 minutes
Serves 6

3 tbsp vegetable or sunflower oil
50 g/1 ¾ oz butter
3 onions, finely chopped
100 g/3 ½ oz/ ½ cup basmati rice,
    rinsed
1 tsp ground blue fenugreek
1 tsp ground marigold
1 tsp ground coriander
1 x 400-g/14-oz can chopped tomatoes
3 garlic cloves, crushed
1 small handful fresh coriander
    (cilantro), leaves chopped, to
    garnish
lemon wedges, to serve

Although this doesn't contain any meat, it contains the unique mix of spices (*kharcho suneli*) that defines the dish. Loaded with cooked rice and tomatoes, this is a substantial dish that would make a meal in its own right. It could even be served as a vegetarian main course as part of a *supra*.

Place the oil and butter in a large pan over a medium heat. Once hot, add the onions and cook, stirring continuously, until soft and just turning golden, about 15 minutes. Add 1 litre/1 ¾ pints/4 cups of boiling water to the pan and then pour in the rice. Bring the pan back to the boil, then stir the rice once and reduce the heat to a simmer. Leave to cook until the rice is tender, about 20 minutes.

Add the spices and tomatoes to the pan and stir to combine. Leave to cook stirring occasionally for another 10 minutes. Add another 500 ml/18 fl oz/2 cups of boiling water to the pan along with the garlic and stir to combine. Cook for 5 minutes more, then divide the soup between serving bowls and garnish with the coriander (cilantro). Serve the soup hot with lemon wedges alongside to squeeze over.

Soup Kharcho

-SPICED BEEF AND RICE SOUP-

Preparation time: 15 minutes
Cooking time: 1 hour 45 minutes
Serves 6

1 kg/2 lb 3 oz boneless beef, cut into
   bite-sized pieces
100 g/3 ½ oz/½ cup basmati rice
50 ml/2 fl oz vegetable or sunflower oil
1 onion, finely chopped
1 x 400-g/14-oz can chopped tomatoes
2 garlic cloves, crushed
½ tsp ground blue fenugreek
½ tsp ground marigold
½ tsp ground coriander
juice of ½ lemon
1 handful fresh coriander (cilantro),
   to garnish
sea salt and chilli powder, to taste

This classic dish gets its name from the fragrant blend of fenugreek, marigold and ground coriander that are used in preparing it, known as *kharcho suneli*. The combination of beef and rice make this hearty soup a meal in its own right.

Place the beef in a large pan and cover with water. Bring just to the boil, then remove from the heat and drain the water. Add 1.4 litres/2 ½ pints of water to the pan and bring back to the boil. Reduce the heat to a simmer and cook, covered, until the meat is almost tender, around 45 minutes.

Add the rice to the pan with the beef and cook for 20 minutes, until the rice and meat are tender.

Meanwhile, heat the oil in a large frying pan (skillet) over a medium heat. Add the onion and cook, stirring continuously, for around 10 minutes, until soft and starting to turn golden. Add the tomatoes, garlic and spices to the pan and cook, stirring, for 5 minutes to allow the flavours to develop.

Add the tomato and onion mixture to the pan with the beef and stir to combine. Bring the mixture back to a simmer and cook for a final 10 minutes. Add the lemon juice to the pan and season to taste.

Ladle the soup into bowls and serve hot.

Bread & Cheese

-CHAPTER 4-

Mchadi

-CORNBREAD-

Preparation time: 20 minutes
Cooking time: 5 minutes
Makes 12 small breads

200 ml/7 fl oz/generous ¾ cup whole
    milk
300 g/10½ oz/2½ cups cornflour (US
    cornstarch) – I use PAN pre-cooked
    white maize meal
2 tbsp vegetable or sunflower oil, plus
    extra for greasing
sea salt

This cornbread hails from west Georgia where it is often simply served with cheese and beans. It requires no proofing and is fried quickly on the stovetop until golden, so it is a wonderfully efficient way of making warm fresh bread.

Pour the milk into a large bowl along with 200 ml/7 fl oz of lukewarm water. Gradually sift the flour into the bowl, incorporating it into the liquid as you go. Once all of the flour has been added, work the dough until it comes together, then turn it out onto a lightly floured surface and knead until firm and smooth. Add the oil and a pinch of salt to the dough and knead again to incorporate.

Lightly grease a large frying pan (skillet) and place it over a medium heat.

Divide the dough into 12 equal-sized pieces and flatten each of them to create an 8-cm/3-inch disc. Working with a few pieces of dough at a time so as not to overcrowd the pan, place the breads into the pan and cook for 3–4 minutes, until lightly golden. Flip onto the other side and cook for another minute, then transfer to a serving plate while you cook the remaining breads.

These are best eaten on the day of making.

Chvishtari

-CORNBREAD WITH CHEESE-

Preparation time: 20 minutes
Cooking time: 5 minutes
Makes 12 small breads

100 ml/3½ fl oz/7 tbsp whole milk
1 egg, beaten
160 g/5¾ oz/1⅓ cups cornflour (US
    cornstarch) – I use PAN pre-cooked
    white maize meal
150 g/5½ oz feta cheese, crumbled
150 g/5½ oz halloumi cheese, grated
vegetable or sunflower oil, for greasing
sea salt

This bread is from Svaneti in north-western Georgia and made in much the same way as the bread on the opposite page, but is enriched with eggs and cheese for a richer result.

Pour the milk into a large bowl along with 200 ml/7 fl oz of tepid water and the beaten egg. Gradually sift the cornflour (cornstarch) into the bowl, incorporating it into the liquid as you go. Once all of the flour has been added, work the dough until it comes together, then turn it out onto a lightly floured surface, pile the cheeses on top and knead to incorporate the cheese and form a firm, smooth dough.

Lightly grease a large frying pan (skillet) and place it over a medium heat.

Divide the dough into 12 equal-size pieces and flatten each of them to create 8-cm/3-inch discs. Working with a few pieces of dough at a time so as not to overcrowd the pan, place the breads into the pan and cook for 3–4 minutes, until lightly golden. Flip onto the other side and cook for another minute, then transfer to a serving plate while you cook the remaining breads.

These are best eaten on the day of making.

Megruli Khachapuri
-DOUBLE CHEESE BREAD-

Preparation time: 2 hours 30 minutes
Cooking time: 10–15 minutes
Makes 6 breads

7g fast-action yeast
1 tsp caster (superfine) sugar
½ tsp fine sea salt
2 eggs and 1 egg yolk
500 ml/18 fl oz whole milk
2 tbsp melted butter
1 kg/2 lb 4 oz plain (all-purpose) flour
4 tbsp sunflower or vegetable oil, plus
    extra for greasing

For the filling:
1 kg/2 lb 4 oz feta, crumbled
500 g/1 lb 2 oz grated mozzarella
100 g/3 ½ oz butter

For the topping:
2 egg yolks
1 tbsp vegetable or sunflower oil

This bread from Megruli is for all the cheese-lovers. The filling is baked into the dough to create a rich mixture of feta and mozzarella cheese, and is then used to cover the bread so you end up with a bubbling, cheesy top!

Preheat the oven to 200°C/400°F/Gas Mark 6 and line 2 large baking sheets with greaseproof paper.

Place the yeast, sugar, salt, eggs and egg yolk in a large mixing bowl and beat to combine. Pour in the milk and whisk well to incorporate, then add the melted butter and whisk again.

Sift the flour into a large bowl or the bowl of a stand mixer fitted with a dough hook. Make a well in the centre of the flour and pour in the milk mixture. Using your hands or the mixer on low, bring the dough together then gradually add the oil to incorporate and continue to knead until smooth. Transfer the dough to a lightly oiled bowl and cover with a damp kitchen cloth. Set aside in a warm place for around 2 hours, until the dough has doubled in size.

Combine the filling ingredients in a large bowl and mix well to combine. Set aside until you are ready to build the breads.

Once the dough has proofed, turn it out onto a lightly floured work surface and knock it back to remove any air bubbles that have developed. Divide into 6 equal-sized pieces and roll each piece into a 20-cm/8-inch round. Reserve one third of the filling mixture to use later and divide the remaining filling between the dough rounds, placing the filling in the centre of each round. Bring up the sides of each round of dough to create a ball and enclose the filling. Pinch the dough together firmly at the top of the ball to seal. Invert the filled dough balls onto your work surface so that they are bottom-side up and press them down firmly to create 20-cm/8-inch rounds (you can use cake pans to achieve even shapes if you prefer).

Mix together the egg yolks and oil for the topping. Transfer the breads to the prepared baking sheets, brush with the topping mixture and top with the reserved filling mixture. Transfer to the oven to bake for 10 minutes, until golden brown and with bubbling cheesy tops. Serve hot.

Imeruli Khachapuri

-IMERULIAN CHEESE BREAD-

Preparation time: 45 minutes
Cooking time: 10–15 minutes
Makes 1 large bread to serve
    6 people

For the dough:

200 g/7 oz/generous 1½ cups plain
    (all-purpose) flour
¼ tsp bicarbonate of soda (baking
    soda)
125 g/4 oz/½ cup low-fat natural
    yogurt
1 egg yolk
pinch of lemon salt
40 g/1½ oz unsalted butter, melted
    and cooled
1 tsp sunflower oil, plus extra for
    greasing

For the filling:

125 g/4½ oz/generous ¾ cup feta
    cheese (preferably Turkish),
    crumbled
125 g/4½ oz/generous 1 cup grated
    mozzarella cheese (buy pre-grated
    cheese as the balls of mozzarella
    are too moist)

To serve:

melted butter, to serve

Perhaps the most iconic of all Georgian dishes, there are as many varieties of cheese bread as there are families in Georgia. I have included other versions later in this book, but, for me, this is the one that reminds me most of home. Because of the importation laws surrounding unpasteurized dairy products, it is impossible to find Imeretian cheese in the UK, and when I first arrived it took me a long time to find an alternative that I was happy with. The combination of feta and mozzarella used here combines to give a lovely salty flavour and melts into tantalizing strings that reveal themselves when you cut into the bread. (**Pictured on page 80.**)

To make the dough, sift the flour and bicarbonate of soda (baking soda) into a large bowl and set aside.

In another large bowl, place the yogurt, egg yolk, lemon salt, melted butter and sunflower oil and mix until combined.

Tip the sifted flour mixture into the wet ingredients and bring together to form a rough dough with your hands, then knead gently until it is smooth and pliable. If the dough sticks to your hands, add a touch more flour.

Lightly grease a clean bowl with sunflower oil and transfer the dough to it. Set aside, covered, for around 30 minutes to allow the dough to rest. Because this is not a yeasted bread, the dough will not rise during this time.

Preheat the oven to 220°C/425°F/gas mark 7 and lightly flour a shallow 23-cm/9-inch round cake pan.

Once the dough has rested, lightly flour a work surface and turn the dough out onto it. Use your hands to flatten the dough into a rough circle, then use a rolling pin to roll it into a large round, around 5-mm/¼-inch thick and roughly the size of the prepared cake pan.

(continues...)

Combine the 2 cheeses for the filling in a bowl, then pile the mixture into the centre of the dough circle, leaving a clear 5-cm/2-inch border of dough around the filling.

Now, working as fast as you can, bring the sides of the dough up over the filling to meet at the top and press the edges together to seal the dough and enclose the cheese. Gently pat the dough to smooth it as much as possible.

Invert the sealed dough ball into the prepared cake pan so that the seam is now on the bottom. Press the dough down to flatten it and spread to the edges of the cake pan; this will ensure that the cheese is spread evenly inside the bread once it is baked.

Place the bread in the preheated oven and leave to cook for 10–15 minutes, until golden brown. Place on a serving platter and brush with the melted butter. Slice into 6 generous pieces and serve warm.

Osuri Khachapuri
-OSSETIAN CHEESE BREAD-

Preparation time: 20 minutes,
   plus 2 hours' proofing time
Cooking time: 15 minutes
Makes 6

7 g/¼ oz fast-action yeast
3 egg yolks
200 ml/7 fl oz/generous ¾ cup milk
1 kg/2 lb 3 oz/8 cups plain (all-
   purpose) flour
1 tsp sugar
4 tbsp soft butter, plus extra for
   greasing
4 tbsp vegetable or sunflower oil, plus
   extra for greasing
8 medium white potatoes, peeled and
   cut into bite-sized chunks
500 g/1 lb 2 oz feta cheese, crumbled
500 g/1 lb 2 oz mozzarella cheese,
   grated
sea salt, to taste

This cheese bread contains yeast and is filled with a mixture of cheese and mashed potato, making it a substantial addition to the dinner table. This recipe makes 6 large breads, each being a meal in its own right. If you want something lighter, halve the recipe and serve it in wedges. You may also wish to bake the breads in batches, re-using just one or two cake pans. (Pictured, top-left on page 81.)

Preheat the oven to 220°C/425°F/gas mark 7 and lightly grease six 20-cm/8-inch cake pans with oil.

Put the yeast in a small bowl and dissolve it in 1 tablespoon of lukewarm water. Beat in the egg yolks and set aside.

Place the milk and 200 ml/7 fl oz water in a large pan over a low heat and heat until lukewarm. Remove from the heat and set aside.

Sift the flour into a large bowl or the bowl of a stand mixer fitted with a dough hook. Add the sugar and butter and use your hands to rub it into the flour until it resembles fine breadcrumbs. Make a well in the centre of the flour and pour in the milk, water, eggs and a quarter of the oil.

Using your hands or the mixer on low, bring the dough together and knead until smooth, gradually adding the remaining oil as you do. Transfer the dough to a lightly oiled bowl and cover with a damp tea (dish) towel. Set aside in a warm place for around 2 hours, until the dough has doubled in size.

Meanwhile, place the potatoes in a large pan and just cover with cold water. Place over a medium heat and bring to the boil, reduce the heat to a simmer and cook for around 15 minutes, until tender. Drain the potatoes, return them to the pan and mash until smooth. Set aside to cool.

(continues...)

Once the potatoes have cooled, add the cheeses to the pan and stir to combine. Season to taste with sea salt and set aside.

Once the dough has proofed, turn it out onto a lightly floured work surface and knock it back to remove any air bubbles that have developed. Divide it into 6 equal-sized pieces and roll each piece into a 20-cm/8-inch round. Place one-sixth of the potato and cheese mixture into the centre of each round of dough and bring up the sides to create a ball and enclose the filling. Pinch the dough together firmly at the top of the ball to seal. Invert the filled dough balls into the prepared cake pans and use your hands to press them down into the pans firmly, spreading them out to fill the base (if you don't have 6 cake pans, this can be done freehand, but this method will help you achieve even shapes).

Snip a hole in the top of each bread and transfer to the oven to cook for 5 minutes, then flip the breads and cook on the reverse side or 5 minutes more.

Remove the breads from the oven and stack them up on a plate, buttering the breads between each layer. Serve warm.

Adjaruli Khachapuri
-ADJARULIAN CHEESE BREAD-

Preparation time: 30 minutes,
    plus 2 hours' proofing time
Cooking time: 20 minutes
Makes 6

7 g/¼ oz fast-action yeast
1 kg/2 lb 3 oz/8 cups plain (all-
    purpose) flour
1 tsp salt
1 tsp sugar
4 tbsp soft butter, plus extra for
    greasing and serving
50 ml/3 tablespoons vegetable or
    sunflower oil, plus extra for greasing
1 kg/2 lb 3 oz feta cheese, crumbled
500 g/1 lb 2 oz mozzarella cheese,
    grated
200 ml/7 fl oz/generous ¾ cup milk
    milk, plus extra for brushing
9 eggs

Of all the Georgian cheese breads, this boat-shaped bread is the most iconic. Adjara is on the Black sea, and boats are a part of everyday life. The egg is said to represent the sun, which sailors navigate by. This is very popular at the Little Georgia, but is very filling so is best shared among a few people. (Pictured, bottom on page 81.)

Place 2 large baking sheets in the oven and preheat to 220°C/425°F/gas mark 7.

Put the yeast in a small bowl and dissolve it in 1 tablespoon of lukewarm water.

Sift the flour into a large bowl or the bowl of a stand mixer fitted with a dough hook. Add the salt, sugar and butter and use your hands to rub it into the flour until it resembles fine breadcrumbs. Make a well in the centre of the flour and pour in 200 ml/7 fl oz lukewarm water, the dissolved yeast and oil.

Using your hands or the mixer on low, bring the dough together and knead until smooth. Transfer the dough to a lightly oiled bowl and cover with a damp tea (dish) towel. Set aside in a warm place for around 2 hours, until the dough has doubled in size.

Place the cheeses in a large bowl and stir to combine. Set aside.

Once the dough has proofed, turn it out onto a lightly floured work surface and knock it back to remove any air bubbles that have developed. Divide it into 6 equal-sized pieces and roll each piece into a 40 x 20-cm/16 x 8-inch oblong. Divide half of the cheese mixture between the centres of the dough rounds and bring up the two sides to make a boat shape and enclose the filling. Pinch the dough together firmly down the central seam to seal. Flip the filled breads over so the seam faces down and use a sharp knife to cut a central seam down the centre of each smooth top, leaving the dough intact at the top and bottom of each oblong. Using your hands, spread the dough from the central seam you have just created.

Mix the milk with the remaining cheese and use this mixture to fill the centre of the breads.

Beat three of the eggs together with 3 tablespoons of milk and use this mixture to brush around the edges of the breads. Transfer to baking sheets and bake in the preheated oven for 10–15 minutes, until almost golden. Remove the breads from the oven and crack an egg into the centre of each, Return to the oven and cook for 2–3 minutes, until the eggs are cooked but still runny. Serve hot, garnished with some butter, if you like.

Guruli Khachapuri
-GURULIAN CHEESE BREAD-

Preparation time: 30 minutes,
    plus 2 hours' proofing time
Cooking time: 25 minutes
Makes 6

7 g/¼ oz fast-action yeast
1 kg/2 lb 3 oz/8 cups plain (all-
    purpose) flour
1 tsp salt
1 tsp sugar
75 g/1¾ oz soft butter, plus extra for
    greasing
350 ml/12 fl oz/scant 1½ cups milk,
    plus extra for brushing
4 tbsp vegetable or sunflower oil, plus
    extra for greasing
10 eggs
1 kg/2 lb 3 oz feta cheese, crumbled
500 g/1 lb 2 oz mozzarella cheese,
    grated

This bread is stuffed with cheese and boiled eggs and folded around its filling much like a Cornish pasty. Like all of the breads in this section, this is very filling so you may want to get your guests to share. (Pictured, top-right on page 81.)

Preheat the oven to 220°C/425°F/gas mark 7.

Place the yeast in a small bowl and dissolve in 1 tablespoon of lukewarm water.

Sift the flour into a large bowl or the bowl of a stand mixer fitted with a dough hook. Add the salt, sugar and butter, a third at a time, and use your hands to rub it into the flour until it resembles fine breadcrumbs. Make a well in the centre of the flour and pour in the milk, dissolved yeast and oil.

Using your hands or the mixer on low, bring the dough together and knead until smooth. Transfer the dough to a lightly oiled bowl and cover with a damp tea (dish) towel. Set aside in a warm place for around 2 hours, until the dough has doubled in size.

Place 7 of the eggs in a large pan and add cold water to cover. Place over a medium heat and bring to the boil. Reduce the heat to a simmer and cook for 9 minutes, until hard boiled. Transfer to a bowl of cold water to cool. Once cool, peel and slice the eggs. Set aside until ready to use.

Place the cheeses in a large bowl and stir to combine. Set aside.

Once the dough has proofed, turn it out onto a lightly floured work surface and knock it back to remove any air bubbles that have developed. Divide it into 6 equal-sized pieces and roll each piece into a 20-cm/8-inch round. Divide the cheese mixture between the dough rounds, then layer the sliced eggs over the top, on one side of the dough circles. Bring over the other side of the dough to enclose the filling and make a half-moon shape. Pinch the dough together firmly at the edges. Brush the tops of the breads with milk and the remaining eggs beaten (as per the recipe on page 84) and transfer to the preheated oven to bake for 10 minutes.

Serve the breads hot, brushed with butter.

Kubdari

-SPICED BEEF AND PORK BREAD-

Preparation time: 40 minutes,
    plus 3 hours' proofing and
    marinating time
Cooking time: 25 minutes
Makes 6

For the dough:
7 g/¼ oz fast-action yeast
3 egg yolks
200 ml/7 fl oz/generous ¾ cup milk
1 kg/2 lb 3 oz/8 cups plain (all-
    purpose) flour
1 tsp sugar
4 tbsp soft butter, plus extra for
    greasing
pinch of sea salt

For the filling:
3 tbsp sunflower or vegetable oil, plus
    extra for greasing
500 g/1 lb 2 oz beef, finely diced
500 g/1 lb 2 oz pork, finely diced
2 tsp ground coriander
1 tsp ground caraway seeds
1 tsp summer savory
½ tsp chilli powder, or to taste
3 onions, finely chopped
2 garlic cloves, crushed
2 tbsp vegetable or sunflower oil
sea salt and freshly ground black
    pepper

This bread is filled with deliciously tender chunks of spiced beef and pork and meltingly soft and sweet onions. This is best served as a meal in its own right, but would also go well with a simple soup or salad alongside.

Preheat the oven to 220°C/425°F/gas mark 7 and lightly grease a 20-cm/8-inch cake pan with oil.

Place the yeast in a small bowl and dissolve it in 1 tablespoon of lukewarm water. Beat in the egg yolks and set aside.

Place the milk and 200 ml/7 fl oz water in a large pan over a low heat and heat until lukewarm. Remove from the heat and set aside.

Sift the flour into a large bowl or the bowl of a stand mixer fitted with a dough hook. Add the sugar, butter and salt, and use your hands to rub it into the flour until it resembles fine breadcrumbs. Make a well in the centre of the flour and pour in the milk, water, eggs and one-quarter of the oil.

Using your hands or the mixer on low, bring the dough together and knead until smooth, gradually adding the remaining oil as you do. Transfer the dough to a lightly oiled bowl and cover with a damp tea (dish) towel. Set aside in a warm place for around 2 hours, until the dough has doubled in size.

While the dough is proofing, prepare the meat filling. Place both types of meat in a large bowl with the spices and mix to combine. Set aside for 1 hour to allow the flavours to develop.

Add the garlic and onions to the meat and use your hands to knead the filling for 20 minutes. This tenderizes the meat and allows the flavours to meld together. Set the filling aside.

(continues...)

Once the dough has proofed, turn it out onto a lightly floured work surface and knock it back to remove any air bubbles that have developed. Divide into 6 equal-sized pieces and roll each piece into a 20-cm/8-inch round. Place one-sixth of the meat and onion mixture into the centre of each round of dough and bring up the sides to create a ball and enclose the filling. Pinch the dough together firmly at the top of the ball to seal. Working with one dough ball at a time, invert the filled balls into the prepared cake pan and use your hands to press them down into the pan firmly, spreading them out to fill the base. Turn the shaped bread out onto the work surface and repeat with the remaining breads, greasing the cake pan between each bread.

Lightly grease a large frying pan (skillet) and place over a high heat. Once hot, reduce the heat to medium and, working with one bread at a time, invert the breads into the pan so that their tops are in contact with the pan's base. Cook for 2–3 minutes, until just golden. Once all the breads have been browned on one side, place them on a baking sheet and transfer them to the oven for 10–15 minutes to finish cooking. Serve hot from the oven.

Kubdari

Spiced beef and pork bread from the valley of Svaneti

The historic region of Svaneti is situated in the north west of Georgia. It is an ancient land famous for its medieval villages and stone towers. Svaneti is amazingly beautiful and mysterious, featuring harsh living conditions and hardy people. The region is famous for producing a kind of salt which is mixed with spices and crushed on a wooden mortar. It is also famous for *kubdari*.

My first memory of this amazing place will always stay with me. We had a family friend who was from Svaneti. One day he said he wanted to take us for a few days' vacation to his homeland, and I was very excited because I had never been to that part of Georgia before. We went by helicopter with a group of friends. When we landed, our friend asked me to walk with him to the house instead of taking the car with the rest of the group. We landed in the most incredible valley, surrounded by mountains on all sides. This big man who had always seemed so strong and unbreakable turned into a little boy who starting gambolling down the hills, touching the trees and telling his childhood stories.

He closed his eyes and walked through the wood towards his house, relying on his memories of the landscape to guide him home. It was as if nature recognised him and welcomed him home. It was the first time in my life that I witnessed such a transformation from a man to a boy.

I spent the most amazing few days there, being introduced to the Svan way of life with its delicious food. I particularly remember *kubdari* and *chvistari*.

On the way back, he asked the pilot if he could co-pilot the helicopter, and the pilot granted his wish (anything is possible in Georgia). On this journey he told us of the legend of Mountain. Deer make their home on this mountain, and there were parts of the landscape where man has never trod. With the pilot's permission, he landed the helicopter on top of the mountain, telling us that it had been his dream since he was very young to reach the top of the mountain. There was a moment when I looked in his eyes and I saw that if he died now he would have no regrets. He returned my stare, smiling, and said 'We fly high. We fly with eagles. Above is only god.'

Gebjalia

-MOZZARELLA, CHILLI AND MINT ROULADE-

Preparation time: 25 minutes
Cooking time: 20 minutes
Serves 4–6

1 litre/1 ¾ pints/4 cups whole milk
1 kg/2 lb 3 oz mozzarella cheese,
    drained and sliced
1 bird's eye chilli, finely chopped
1 tsp sea salt
1 bunch fresh mint, leaves chopped
500 g/1 lb 2 oz ricotta cheese
200 g/7 oz/1 scant cup sour cream

The technique required to make this dish can take time to master because it requires a certain amount of feel and intuition. Do persevere though, as the reward is more than worth the effort, and the alchemy of transforming mozzarella and milk into something new is still thrilling to me, despite having been making this dish for years. The subtle, milky flavour of the mozzarella is cut through with a fiery mint and chilli paste that can be adjusted to suit your tastes.

Put the milk in a large pan over a medium heat. When the milk starts to steam, turn the heat to low and add the mozzarella cheese to the pan. Continue to heat, stirring continuously, until the cheese comes together into a large, stringy ball. Strain the pan through a sieve (strainer) into a bowl, saving the leftover milk to use later. Transfer the cheese ball to a lightly greased chopping board and roll it out to a thickness of 5 mm/¼ inch, being careful that it does not break. Set aside.

Put the chilli, salt and three-quarters of the mint in a large mortar and grind with a pestle to a smooth paste. Spread this paste over the mozzarella to just coat, reserving the leftover paste to use later. Working from one of the widest edges, roll the cheese as tightly as you can to create a long cylinder. Set aside.

Put the ricotta cheese, sour cream and a little of the leftover milk in a large bowl and use an electric whisk to beat until smooth, adding more milk if the mixture is too thick. Add the remaining mint paste to the mixture and beat again to incorporate. Transfer to a large, shallow serving platter.

Slice the rolled mozzarella into 5-cm/2-inch rounds. Spoon 1–2 tablespoons of the sauce onto plates and place a few of the rolled mozzarella rounds, spiral-side up, in the sauce. Scatter over the remaining mint leaves and serve.

Nadugi

-RICOTTA WITH MINT AND CHILLI-

Preparation time: 15 minutes
Cooking time: N/A
Serves 4–6

10–30 g/½–1 oz fresh mint leaves,
    chopped
1 green chilli, finely chopped
½ tsp coarse sea salt
500 g/1 lb 2 oz ricotta cheese
125 ml/4 fl oz/generous ½ cup sour
    cream

This creamy combination of ricotta cheese and sour cream is cut through by a
vibrant paste of chilli and mint. It's delicious spread over bread or alongside
a plateful of other salads, but it can also be used to fill cones of mozzarella and
served as a moreish canapé.

Place the mint, chilli and salt in a mortar and grind with a pestle to form a
smooth paste. Set aside.

Place the ricotta in a large bowl and stir to combine. Add the sour cream and
stir to form a smooth, hummus-like consistency. Add the mint paste and stir
until just combined. Serve.

Optional: Roll sliced mozzarella squares into cone shapes and tie with chive
sprigs to secure. Fill the cones with the *Nadugi* mixture and serve.

Gomi

-SAVOURY PORRIDGE-

Preparation time: 5 minutes, plus
    1 hour's resting time
Cooking time: 45 minutes
Serves 6

500 g/1 lb 2 oz short-grain rice, rinsed
½ tsp butter
sea salt and freshly ground black
    pepper

This simple rice porridge may seem bland to some palates, but it makes an
excellent foil for dishes that are rich with spice. Traditionally made with
cornmeal, it is often served at a *supra* alongside the cheese dishes, and Nadugi
(above) is a wonderful example of this. It works well to offset their salty
richness.

Place the rice in a large pan with 3 litres/5 ¼ pints of water. Place over a high
heat and bring just to the boil, then remove the pan from the heat and leave to
rest, covered, for 1 hour.

Once the rice has rested, remove the lid and place over a very low heat. Leave to
cook, stirring occasionally, for 30–40 minutes, until the rice has broken down
to a thick porridge-like (oatmeal-like) consistency. Add the butter to the pan
and stir until it has melted through, then season to taste. Serve hot.

Shemzvari Sulguni

-FRIED SULGUNI 2 WAYS-

A friend of mine owns a hotel in the Kakheti (east Georgia) called Chateau Mere, and is always sending me recipes that her team create in the restaurant. Fried sulguni is a common dish in Georgia but this recipe has a twist in that it uses basil and tarragon. In Georgia, this would be made with sulguni, a brined cheese with a salty and slightly sour flavour but, because of the limitations on the importation of unpasteurized cheese, it is nearly impossible to get sulguni in the UK. Halloumi makes an excellent substitute. I prepare this in two ways, one soft and melty and the other with a bit of crunch. I can't pick between them so have decided to share both with you here.

1. SHALLOW-FRIED SULGUNI WITH FRESH HERBS

Preparation time: 10 minutes
Cooking time: 10 minutes
Serves 4–6

3 tbsp vegetable or sunflower oil
600 g/1 lb 5 oz halloumi cheese, thinly sliced
1 small handful fresh tarragon, leaves chopped
1 small handful fresh basil, leaves torn
2 spring onions (scallions), sliced
2 garlic cloves, crushed

Place the oil in a large frying pan (skillet) over a medium heat. Once hot, add the halloumi to the pan and cook on one side for around 3 minutes, until golden.

Flip the halloumi in the pan to cook the other side, then scatter over the fresh herbs, spring onions (scallions) and garlic. Cover the pan and leave to cook, covered, for 3 minutes, until soft and golden on both sides.

I like to place the hot pan in the middle of the table and let everyone dig in, but you could transfer to a serving plate if you prefer.

2. HERB-STUFFED SULGUNI WITH CRISPY BREADCRUMBS

Preparation time: 30 minutes
Cooking time: 10 minutes
Serves 4–6

600 g/1 lb 5 oz halloumi cheese, cut
   into bite-sized triangular wedges
   – try to source very light, low-salt
   halloumi cheese if possible
1 small handful fresh tarragon, leaves
   chopped
1 small handful fresh basil, leaves torn
2 eggs, beaten, in a bowl
100 g/3 ½ oz panko breadcrumbs, in
   a bowl
3 tbsp vegetable or sunflower oil

Using a sharp knife, cut a deep pocket into the longest edge of each of the wedges of halloumi, then stuff with a mixture of the fresh herbs. Set aside.

Put the bowl of beaten eggs and the bowl of breadcrumbs on a work surface. Then, working with one piece of cheese at a time, dip the cheese into the egg and then roll in the breadcrumbs. Transfer to a plate while you finish the rest of the cheese. Transfer the prepared cheese to the fridge to rest for 15 minutes, but do not discard the bowls of egg and breadcrumbs as you will need them again.

Once the cheese has rested, remove it from the fridge and place it on the work surface next to the eggs and breadcrumbs. Again, working with one wedge at a time, dip the cheese in the egg one more time followed by the breadcrumbs. This double coating ensures that the breadcrumb coating is extra crispy once the cheese is fried. Set aside.

Place the oil in a large frying pan (skillet) over a medium heat. Once hot, add the halloumi to the pan and cook for 2 minutes on each side, until all the edges are golden and crispy. Transfer to a serving plate and serve hot.

Meat Dishes

-CHAPTER 5-

Kebabi

-LAMB KEBABS-

Preparation time: 20 minutes
Cooking time: 20 minutes
Serves 6

For the kebabi:
1 tbsp plus 1 tsp vegetable or
    sunflower oil
2 medium onions, finely chopped
500 g/1 lb 2 oz minced (ground) lamb
2 garlic cloves, crushed, then minced
    to a paste using a pestle and mortar
1 tbsp dried basil
½ tbsp dried mint
1 large handful coriander (cilantro)
    leaves, chopped
1 tsp finely ground black pepper
½ tsp chilli powder
1 tsp sea salt
1 tsp tomato purée (paste), dissolved
    in 1 tbsp boiled and cooled water
¼ tsp ground caraway seeds

To serve:
3 large round lavash (flatbreads) or
    tortillas, sliced in half
3 tbsp pomegranate molasses or 3 tsp
    Ajika of your choice (Chilli Paste,
    see pages 28–31)
1 large handful fresh parsley, chopped
1 red onion, finely sliced
6 tbsp pomegranate seeds

Wrapped in soft pillowy *lavash* (flatbread), these delicious lamb kebabs make a great portable snack, so they're ideal for cooking at a barbecue or to make ahead as part of a picnic or packed lunch. I like to serve these open with the various toppings and garnishes on the side for people to assemble themselves.

Preheat the oven to 200°C/400°F/gas mark 6 and line a large baking sheet with parchment paper.

To make the *kebabi*, heat 1 teaspoon of the oil in a frying pan (skillet) over a medium heat, then add the onion and cook for 5 minutes until soft and just starting to colour. Set aside to cool to room temperature.

Once the onions have cooled, place all of the other ingredients for the *kebabi* in a large bowl, then use your hands to mix through and ensure everything is thoroughly combined. Form the mixture into a ball, then pick it up with your hands and bring it back down into the bowl with some force; repeat this several times — I find this distributes the ingredients well throughout the mixture.

Wash and lightly oil your hands to prevent the mixture from sticking, then divide the mixture into 6 even-sized balls. Form the balls into fat sausage shapes with your hands, roughly the length of a halved *lavash* or tortilla.

Heat the remaining oil in a frying pan (skillet) over a medium heat, then add the *kebabi* to the pan and turn until nicely coloured on all sides. Do this in batches to avoid overcrowding the pan. Once the *kebabi* are nicely coloured, transfer them to the prepared baking sheet and set aside while you finish the others. Transfer the *kebabi* to the preheated oven for 18–20 minutes to finish cooking.

To serve the *kebabi*, divide the halved *lavash* or tortilla among 6 serving plates and spread each with your choice of pomegranate molasses or *Ajika*. Allow your guests to garnish their kebabs with fresh parsley, sliced red onion and pomegranate seeds before rolling and enjoying hot.

Chanakhi

-LAMB STEW WITH AUBERGINE-

Preparation time: 40 minutes
Cooking time: 2 hours
Serves 6

1 kg/2 lb 3 oz aubergines (eggplants),
approximately 3 medium aubergines
6 onions
6 garlic cloves, crushed
3 fresh green chillies, finely chopped,
or to taste
1 kg/2 lb 3 oz lamb shoulder, finely
diced
2 tbsp dried basil
2 tbsp dried summer savory
3 tbsp vegetable or sunflower oil
2 red (bell) peppers, halved and sliced
into half rings
3 medium white potatoes, peeled and
cut into 2.5-cm/1-inch cubes
3 x 400-g/14-oz cans chopped
tomatoes
3 celery stalks, finely chopped
1 small handful fresh parsley, leaves
chopped
plain boiled rice, to serve
sea salt and chilli powder, to taste

This dish takes its name from the clay pot that it was traditionally cooked in.
Though I have called it a stew, it actually starts off as a lamb-stuffed aubergine
that breaks down and melds with the sauce on account of its long cooking time.
It is a little fiddly to prepare, but well worth the effort and can be made ahead
of time and left to bubble away in the oven for a couple of hours while you are
getting on with other things.

Preheat the oven to 200°C/400°F/gas mark 6.

Slice off the tops and bases of the aubergines (eggplants) and discard, then slice
the aubergines in half horizontally to create squat cylinders. Use a spoon to
hollow out the aubergine halves, retaining the flesh and being careful not to go
all the way through the base of the aubergine. Set aside.

Finely chop 3 of the onions and place in a bowl with the garlic, chilli and lamb
and mix to combine. Finely chop the flesh from the centre of the aubergines
along with the dried basil and summer savory, then season generously and mix
again to combine. Spoon this mixture into the hollowed-out aubergines and
set aside.

Pour the oil into the base of a large rectangular roasting pan. Halve and finely
slice the remaining onions and lay over the base of the pan. Scatter over half of
the red (bell) pepper and sit the filled aubergines on top, packing them in snugly
so that they don't fall over during cooking. Scatter over the potatoes, pressing
them down between any gaps in the aubergines and set aside.

Place the tomatoes, celery and parsley in a bowl and mix to combine. Season
with sea salt and chilli powder, then pour the mixture over the aubergines in the
roasting pan.

Cover the dish with foil and transfer to the oven to cook for 1½ –2 hours, until
the lamb is tender and fragrant. Serve hot with plain boiled rice.

Kayrma

-LAMB IN POMEGRANATE-

Preparation time: 10 minutes
Cooking time: 40 minutes
Serves 6

100 ml/3 ½ fl oz vegetable or
   sunflower oil
1 kg/2 lb 3 oz boneless lamb shoulder,
   cut into bite-sized pieces
2 bay leaves
1 kg/2 lb 3 oz onions, halved and
   finely sliced
3 garlic cloves, crushed
juice of 1 large pomegranate
sea salt and chilli powder, to taste
plain boiled rice or bread, to serve

Pomegranate juice imparts a lovely flavour to this dish which is halfway between sweet and sour. If you don't want to juice your own pomegranate, you could use store-bought juice, but doing it yourself, in the same way as you would juice a lemon, is far more economical and rewarding.

Place half of the oil in a large pan over a medium heat. Once hot, add the lamb and bay leaves and cook, stirring continuously, for 10 minutes, until the lamb is almost tender.

In another large pan, heat the remaining oil over a medium heat. Once hot, add the onions and cook, stirring continuously, until soft and just golden, about 10–15 minutes. Add the garlic to the pan and cook for 2 minutes more.

Add the lamb to the pan with the onions and stir to combine. Pour over the pomegranate juice and stir to combine. Bring the mixture to the boil, then reduce to a simmer and cook for 5–10 minutes more.

Remove the bay leaves from the pan and season to taste. Transfer to serving plates and serve with plain boiled rice or bread.

Chakapuli

-LAMB STEW WITH SOUR PLUMS-

Preparation time: 20 minutes
Cooking time: 40 minutes
Serves 6

1 tbsp vegetable or sunflower oil
1 kg/2 lb 3 oz boneless lamb shoulder,
   cut into bite-sized pieces
2 onions, finely chopped
2 bay leaves
2 bunches spring onions (scallions),
   finely sliced
1 handful fresh coriander (cilantro),
   chopped
1 handful fresh parsley, chopped
1 handful fresh tarragon, chopped
70 g/2½ oz garlic scapes, chopped
2 green chillies, finely chopped
250 g/9 oz sour green plums, peeled
   and pitted, or the juice of 2 limes
450 ml/16 fl oz dry white wine
lavash (flatbread), to serve

Sour plums only have a short season and can be hard to find in the UK, although sometimes I am lucky enough to spot some at the specialist Middle Eastern grocers that are local to me. The plums melt into the sauce adding a beautifully rich sourness, so they are well worth seeking out. Otherwise, lime juice makes a great substitute and will still yield a rich, unctuous and pleasingly sour sauce.

Heat the oil in a large pan over a medium heat. Once hot, add the lamb to the pan and cook, stirring, until just browned. Add the chopped onions and cook, stirring, for around 10 minutes, until the meat is almost tender, adding a splash of water to the pan if it is too dry.

Add the bay leaves, spring onions (scallions), coriander, parsley, tarragon, garlic scapes and chillies to the pan and cook, stirring, for another 10 minutes. If the mixture is too dry (it should be juicy but not liquid), add a splash of water.

Add the plums to the pan (if using), and stir to combine. Now add the wine and cook, half covered, until the alcohol has cooked off, around 10 minutes. If you haven't used plums, add the lime juice and season to taste.

Serve warm with *lavash* (flatbread) alongside for mopping up the juices.

Cxvris Chashushuli

-LAMB AND POTATO STEW-

Preparation time: 25 minutes
Cooking time: 1 hour
Serves 4–6

4 tbsp vegetable or sunflower oil
1 kg/2 lb 3 oz boneless lamb shoulder,
    cut into bite-sized pieces
6 onions, halved and finely sliced
1 large bunch fresh coriander
    (cilantro), leaves separated and
    stems chopped
6 medium white potatoes, peeled and
    cut into wedges
3 x 400-g/14-oz cans chopped
    tomatoes
4 garlic cloves, crushed
1 fresh green chilli, finely chopped,
    or to taste
sea salt and chilli powder, to taste

This rich lamb and potato stew is a variation of a traditional dish that is made with pheasant or chicken. Here, potatoes are added to the lamb, which breaks down and thickens the tomato sauce during cooking. This is a robust dish that is packed with flavour and would be equally at home at a feast or a casual mid-week family meal.

Place the oil in a large pan over a medium heat. Once hot, add the lamb, onions and coriander (cilantro) stalks and cook, stirring continuously, until the meat is browned. Add the potatoes and continue to cook, stirring occasionally, until almost tender, about 15 minutes. Add the chopped tomatoes to the pan and stir to combine. Cook for another 15 minutes, stirring occasionally.

Place most of the coriander leaves, garlic, chilli and a pinch of salt in a mortar and grind to a paste with a pestle. Add this paste to the pan with the lamb and potatoes and stir to combine. Cook for 5 minutes more, then season to taste with sea salt and chilli powder and transfer to a serving dish and garnish with the remaining coriander. Serve hot.

Chashushuli

-BEEF STEW-

Preparation time: 25 minutes
Cooking time: 1 hour 15 minutes
Serves 4–6

5 tbsp vegetable or sunflower oil
50 g/1¾ oz butter
1 tsp ground caraway seeds
4 allspice berries
1 kg/2 lb 3 oz good-quality stewing
   beef, cut into bite-sized pieces
3 onions, halved and finely sliced
1 red chilli, finely chopped, or to taste
1 tbsp tomato purée (paste)
1½ tsp brown sugar
1 x 400-g/14-oz can chopped tomatoes
3 garlic cloves, crushed
1 small handful fresh coriander
   (cilantro), leaves chopped
1 small handful fresh basil, leaves torn

In this stew, dense with the flavour of tomatoes, garlic and coriander (cilantro), the beef is cooked until it is beautifully soft and tender. The toasted caraway seeds and allspice berries give the sauce a great depth of flavour. It is also lifted by the sweetness of the slow-cooked onions.

Place half of the oil and half of the butter in a large pan over a medium heat. Once hot, add the ground caraway seeds, allspice berries and the beef. Stir to coat the beef in the spices, then cook, stirring continuously, until the meat is browned. Add the onions and chilli to the pan and continue to cook, stirring occasionally, for 30–40 minutes, until the meat is almost tender. If the pan starts to look too dry, add the remaining butter and oil to the pan.

Meanwhile heat a small pan over a medium heat and add the tomato purée (paste) and sugar. Cook, stirring continuously, until the tomato has thickened and darkened slightly in colour, then add the chopped tomatoes and stir to combine. Leave to cook until just bubbling, then add this mixture to the pan with the beef and stir to combine.

Add the garlic and fresh herbs to the pan and season to taste. Cook for a couple of minutes more to allow the flavours to develop. Serve hot.

Sakonlis Khorzis Kharcho

-SPICED BEEF AND WALNUT STEW-

Preparation time: 15 minutes
Cooking time: 50 minutes
Serves 4–6

1 kg/2 lb 3 oz. boneless beef,
    cut into bite-sized pieces
200 g/7 oz walnuts
3 garlic cloves
1 tsp ground coriander
1 tsp dried ground marigold
1 tsp ground cinnamon
½ tsp ground cloves
pinch of nutmeg
1-2 tbsp vegetable oil
3 onions, finely chopped
50 g/1 ¾ oz fresh coriander (cilantro),
    leaves picked and stems chopped
2 bay leaves
2 egg yolks
1 tbsp vinegar
sea salt and chilli powder, to taste
Gomi (Rice Pudding, see page 93), rice
    or bread, to serve

This is a classic Georgian dish that contains the special spice blend of marigold, coriander and cinnamon. Walnuts and egg yolks are added to the sauce, making it especially rich and unctuous. This is Georgia on a plate.

Place the beef in a large pan and cover with 1.5 litres/3 ¼ pints water. Bring just to the boil over a medium heat, then remove from the heat and skim off any scum from the surface of the water. Return to the heat and bring back to the boil, reduce the heat to a simmer and cook until just tender, about 20 minutes.

Meanwhile, place the walnuts in a food processor and process to a very fine paste. The paste should be sticky and smooth, but not at all grainy (this can take up to 5 minutes).

Crush the garlic with the back of a knife and then put in a mortar with a pinch of sea salt. Grind with a pestle to a smooth paste. Add to the walnut paste with the ground coriander, marigold, cinnamon, cloves and nutmeg and stir to combine. Set aside until needed.

Once the meat is cooked, drain through a sieve (strainer) set over a large bowl, reserving the liquid. Return the beef to the pan with 1–2 tablespoons of the reserved liquid and the oil. Add the onions and coriander (cilantro) stems and cook, stirring, for 15 minutes, until the onions are tender.

Dissolve the walnut and garlic paste in the reserved liquid, add the bay leaves and then add the mixture to the pan with the beef. Bring to the boil, then reduce the heat to a simmer and leave to cook for 15 minutes to allow the flavours to develop. Then remove the pan from the heat to cool for 3–4 minutes. Remove the bay leaves and discard.

Beat the egg yolks and vinegar together in a small bowl, then stir through the beef. Return the pan to the heat and cook, stirring continuously, for 4 minutes. Season to taste with sea salt and chilli powder and stir through the coriander leaves. Serve hot with *Gomi*, rice or bread.

Abkhazura

-SPICED PORK AND BEEF MEATBALLS-

Preparation time: 30 minutes
Cooking time: 15 minutes
Serves 4–6

500 g/1 lb 2 oz minced (ground) pork
500 g/1 lb 2 oz minced (ground) beef
3 onions, finely chopped
5 garlic cloves, crushed
1 tsp chilli powder
1 tsp ground coriander
2 tsp dried summer savory
1 tsp ground blue fenugreek (optional)
1 tbsp sumac (optional)
500 g/1 lb 2 oz caul fat
2 tbsp vegetable or sunflower oil
sliced raw red onion and pomegranate
    seeds, to garnish

These meaty parcels from western Georgia are full of flavour and deliciously juicy. The meat is wrapped with caul fat, the membrane that surrounds the internal organs of cows, sheep and pigs, which helps to give shape and creates a deliciously crisp outer coating.

If you have a meat mincer, pass the pork, beef and onions through together to fully combine. If not, place the onions in a food processor and briefly pulse, until very fine, but not watery.

Place the pork, beef and onions in a large bowl and add the garlic and all of the spices. Using your hands, work the spices through the meat to ensure they are well incorporated.

Lay the caul fat out flat and slice into 15 x 20-cm/6 x 8-inch rectangles. Place a large spoonful of the meat mixture in the centre of each rectangle of fat, then fold the edges over to fully enclose the meat.

Heat the oil in a large frying pan (skillet) over a medium heat. Once hot, add the wrapped parcels and cook, turning occasionally, for around 10 minutes, until golden all over and cooked through.

Transfer to a serving platter and garnish with the slices of red onion and the pomegranate seeds.

Khinkali

-BEEF AND PORK DUMPLINGS-

Preparation time: 45 minutes
Cooking time: 10–15 minutes
Serves 4–6

For the dough:
500 g/1 lb 2 oz plain (all-purpose)
    flour
1 egg, beaten
1 tsp salt
200 ml/7 fl oz distilled water

For the filling:
500 g/1 lb 2 oz coarsely minced
    (ground) beef
500 g/1 lb 2 oz coarsely minced
    (ground) pork
3 onions, very finely chopped
¼ tsp ground caraway seeds
½ tsp ground black pepper
1 tsp fine sea salt
¼ tsp ground allspice

To serve:
sea salt and freshly ground black
    pepper, to taste
chilli powder, sour cream or crème
    fraîche (optional)

The boys that I grew up with used to take great pride in polishing off enormous platefuls of these moreish dumplings and, truth be told, so did I. When eating them, you pick them up by their stalks, bite off the meat-filled pocket and discard the doughy nubbin. The problem with this is that it is easy for people to keep track of how many you have eaten and, growing up, I had always eaten more than was deemed delicate or feminine! Not wanting to miss out on my favourite food, I remember going to great lengths to conceal the giveaway pieces of dough in my pockets when on dates as a teenager. Luckily times have moved on and I am now free to devour as many of these as I choose.

To make the filling, place all the ingredients in a large bowl and use your hands to combine. Transfer to the fridge, covered, for 30 minutes to let the flavours develop. Once the meat has rested, you can quickly fry off a small spoonful of the filling to test the seasoning if you like.

While the filling is resting, make the dough. Sift the flour into a large bowl and make a well in the centre. Add the egg, salt and water to the well and then use your hands to form a rough dough. Turn out onto a lightly floured surface and knead gently until the dough is just smooth, then set aside to rest for 30 minutes.

Once rested, place the dough on a lightly-floured surface and roll out to a thickness of 5 mm/¼ inch. Using a 10 cm/4 in round pastry cutter, cut circles from the dough. Then reroll the offcuts and use up the remaining dough.

Working with one piece of dough at a time, place 1 tablespoon of the filling in the centre of each dough circle. To shape the dumplings, work around the circumference of the dough circle to bring the dough up around the filling. Pleat it like an accordion as you go – the pleats will eventually come together to encase the filling and leave a central stalk.

Once you have finished all the dumplings, bring a large pan of salted water to a simmer. Being careful not to overcrowd the pan, drop the dumplings into the water top-side down and leave to cook, covered, for 10–15 minutes, until the dumplings are floating on the surface of the water. Be careful not to cook them for too long as this can cause them to fall apart.

Drain the dumplings and transfer to a serving dish, then season with salt and pepper. Traditionally these are served as they are with a little chilli powder sprinkled over the top, but they are also delicious with a generous spoonful of sour cream or crème fraîche served alongside.

Kupati

-SPICED GEORGIAN SAUSAGE-

Preparation time: 15 minutes
Cooking time: 10 minutes
Serves 4–6

1 kg/2 lb 4 oz minced (ground) pork
   loin
2 onions, finely chopped
3 garlic cloves, crushed
1 tsp dried ground marigold
1 tsp ground coriander
1 tsp ground blue fenugreek
1½ tsp summer savory
chilli powder, to taste
1 whole egg and 1 egg yolk
100 ml/3½ oz vegetable or sunflower
   oil
100 g/3½ oz pomegranate seeds
sea salt and freshly ground black
   pepper
Mchadi (Cornbread, see page 36) and
   Tkemali (Plum Sauce, see page 22),
   to serve

In Georgia these are traditionally made with pig's heart, liver, kidneys and intestines, and the process of making them is very fiddly and time-consuming. As this is one of my favourite dishes, when I first opened Little Georgia, I was determined to serve them in the traditional way but, because people in the UK were less accustomed to eating offal than back home in Georgia, they did not sell well. In the restaurant, I now make them with minced (ground) pork loin and they are very popular. This is the recipe I am sharing with you here.

If you have a mincer, pass the meat through it with the onions, garlic and the herbs and spices. If not, place the same ingredients in a food processor and pulse until smooth. Transfer the mixture to a large bowl and add the egg and extra yolk, using your hands to combine. Form the mixture into sausage shapes and set aside.

Heat the oil in large frying pan (skillet) over a medium heat. Once hot, add the *kupati* and fry, turning occasionally, until golden brown and cooked through. This should take approximately 10 minutes.

Transfer the *kupati* to a serving plate and garnish with the pomegranate seeds. Serve hot with *Mchadi* and *Tkemali*.

Kupati

Memories of spiced Georgian sausage

My love for *kupati* started when I was little. We had a large holiday house in Abkhazia, on the eastern coast of the Black Sea. One summer, my grandmother took me to visit one of her friends who lived nearby, and while they were chatting and preparing food, I played outside with the neighbourhood children. Suddenly, my play was interrupted by a totally alien smell that was smoky, spicy and totally irresistible. Like a sniffing dog, I followed my nose and chased the delicious aroma all the way back to the kitchen, where I found the table set for lunch and my grandmother and her friend waiting for me. The anticipation caused by the incredible smell of the piping hot *kupati* and the sound of them sizzling in the pan had me drooling, and the taste was even more heavenly. This memory is forever imprinted on my senses and whenever I smell *kupati* cooking, I am a child once again.

Goris Khorzis Mtsvadi

-PORK WITH POMEGRANATE-

Preparation time: 20 minutes,
    plus at least 4 hours' soaking and
    marinating time
Cooking time: 30 minutes
Serves 4

1 kg/2 lb 3 oz pork neck fillet, cut into
    bite-sized chunks
1½ tbsp apple cider vinegar or white
    wine vinegar
1 tsp *Ziteli Ajika* (Red Chilli Paste, see
    page 30)
2 onions, halved and thickly sliced
juice of 1 pomegranate
vegetable or sunflower oil, for greasing
sea salt and freshly ground black
    pepper, to taste
lavash (flatbread) and *Tkemali* (Plum
    Sauce, see page 22), to serve

This rustic dish features tender chunks of pork and pink onions infused with the sweetness of pomegranates. It is traditionally cooked over an open fire or hot charcoals, so you could barbecue the meat if you like. Wrapped in *lavash* with plum sauce generously spooned over, this dish is simple to prepare but packs a real flavour punch that is hot, sweet and sour all at the same time.

Place the pork in a large baking dish.

In a small bowl, combine the vinegar and *Ajika*, then spoon this mixture over the pork. Using your hands, turn the pork in the sauce to ensure it is well coated. Cover with clingfilm (plastic wrap) and transfer to the fridge to marinate for at least 2 hours or overnight.

Meanwhile, lay the onion rings in a flat dish and pour over the pomegranate juice. Leave to soak for at least 30 minutes, then use your hands to squeeze and break up the onions.

Preheat the oven to 200°C/400°F/gas mark 6 and grease a large baking sheet with the oil.

Lay the marinated pork on the prepared baking sheet and season with salt and pepper. Cover with foil and transfer to the preheated oven for 15–20 minutes, until tender, removing the foil for the last 5 minutes of cooking.

Serve the pork on *lavash* with the onions spooned over the top and with *Tkemali* on the side.

Neknebi

-PORK RIBS-

Preparation time: 25 minutes, plus at
    least 2 hours' marinating time
Cooking time: 1 hour
Serves 4

1 tsp *Ziteli Ajika* (Red Chilli Paste, see
    page 30)
2 tbsp apple cider vinegar or white
    wine vinegar
4 tbsp vegetable or sunflower oil,
    plus extra for greasing
1 rack baby back pork ribs
2 onions, halved and finely sliced
4 tbsp tomato purée (paste)
2 tsp caster (superfine) sugar
2 egg yolks
1 tsp ground cinnamon
¼ tsp ground cloves
2 garlic cloves, crushed
pinch of nutmeg
chilli powder, to taste
1 handful fresh coriander (cilantro),
    leaves chopped
sea salt and freshly ground black
    pepper

Here, pork ribs are cooked until delectably soft and falling off the bone and
slathered in a rich and sticky spiced tomato sauce that is sure to have your guests
coming back for more. Like many cheaper cuts of meat, all these ribs need is a
little care and low and slow cooking to become meltingly tender.

Preheat the oven to 200°C/400°F/gas mark 6 and lightly oil a large roasting pan.

Place the *Ajika*, 1 tablespoon of the vinegar and 2 tablespoons of the oil in
a bowl and mix to combine. Place the ribs in a large baking dish and pour
over the sauce, using your hands to ensure the ribs are well coated. Cover with
clingfilm (plastic wrap) and transfer to the fridge to marinate for at least 2 hours
or overnight.

Once marinated, place the ribs in the prepared roasting pan and drizzle over any
residual marinade. Add 1 tablespoon of boiling water to the pan and cover with
foil. Transfer to the preheated oven to cook for 30 minutes, then remove the foil
and cook for another 30 minutes, adding more water if the ribs look too dry.

Meanwhile, heat the remaining oil in a large frying pan (skillet) over a medium
heat. Once hot, add the onions and cook, stirring continuously, until soft and
just turning golden, around 10 minutes. Using a wooden spoon or spatula, push
the onions to the side of the pan. Add the tomato purée (paste) and sugar to
the centre of the pan and cook, stirring, for around 2 minutes, until thickened.
Combine the onions in the pan with the tomato, then add 5 tablespoons of
boiling water and stir to combine — add more water if the mixture looks too
thick. Leave to simmer for 5 minutes.

Meanwhile, beat the egg yolks with the remaining tablespoon of vinegar until
combined. Set aside.

Remove the pan containing the tomato and onion mixture from the heat
and allow to cool for 3–4 minutes. Mix the eggs through the tomato mixture
and return the pan to the heat, stirring continuously, for 3 minutes. Add the
cinnamon, cloves, garlic, nutmeg and chilli powder, stir to combine and season
to taste. Continue to cook, stirring occasionally, for 5 minutes to allow the
flavours to develop.

Slice the rack of ribs into individual ribs and place on a serving platter. Pour
over the sauce and garnish with the coriander (cilantro) leaves. Serve hot.

Mtsvadis Chashushuli

-PORK STEW-

Preparation time: 30 minutes, plus at
  least 2 hours' marinating time
Cooking time: 20 minutes
Serves 4

1 kg/2 lb 3 oz pork neck fillet, cut into
  bite-sized chunks
1½ tbsp apple cider vinegar or white
  wine vinegar
1 tsp *Ziteli Ajika* (Red Chilli Paste, see
  page 30)
20 g/¾ oz butter
2 tbsp vegetable or sunflower oil, plus
  extra for greasing
4 onions, halved and finely sliced
3 tbsp tomato purée (paste)
1½ tsp brown sugar
sea salt and freshly ground black
  pepper
plain boiled rice, to serve

The pork in this dish is cooked in the same way as the *Goris Khorzis Mtsvadi* (Pork with Pomegranate, see page 116), but here it is added to a tomato and onion sauce for a more substantial dish. If you like spice, you could add an extra spoonful of *Ajika* to the sauce just before serving.

Place the pork in a large baking dish.

In a small bowl, combine the vinegar and *Ajika*, then spoon this mixture over the pork. Using your hands, turn the meat in the sauce to ensure it is well coated. Cover with clingfilm (plastic wrap) and transfer to the fridge to marinate for at least 2 hours or overnight.

Preheat the oven to 200°C/400°F/gas mark 6 and grease a large baking sheet with the oil.

Lay the marinated pork on the prepared baking sheet and season with salt and pepper. Cover with foil and transfer to the preheated oven for 15–20 minutes, until tender, removing the foil for the last 5 minutes of cooking.

While the pork is cooking, heat the butter and oil in a large frying pan (skillet) over a medium heat. Once hot, add the onions and cook, stirring continuously, until soft and just turning golden, about 10 minutes. Using a wooden spoon or spatula, push the onions to the side of the pan and add the tomato purée (paste) and brown sugar to the centre of the pan. Cook the tomato and sugar mixture for a couple of minutes, until slightly thickened, and then stir the onions through the tomatoes.

Remove the pork from the oven and add it to the pan with the tomato and onion mixture. Stir everything to combine and leave to cook, covered, for 7–8 minutes, until fragrant and bubbling. Serve the pork hot with plain boiled rice.

Right: My family gathered around the table, enjoying the food, wine and debate that are essential to supra.

Poultry Dishes

-CHAPTER 6-

Satsivi

-TURKEY IN WALNUT SAUCE-

Preparation time: 40 minutes, plus
   resting time
Cooking time: 2 hours 30 minutes
Serves 6

1 medium turkey (approximately
   6 kg/13 lb 4 oz)
250 g/9 oz/1¾ cups walnut halves
4 garlic cloves
1 tsp ground coriander
1 tsp ground marigold
1 tsp ground blue fenugreek
3 onions, finely chopped
1 tsp ground cinnamon
½ tsp ground cloves
2 eggs
1 tbsp apple cider vinegar or white
   wine vinegar
sea salt, to taste

This recipe is the Georgian version of Christmas turkey. My great grandparents used to make this a couple of days ahead and leave it suspended in a well in their garden until it was ready to be served.

Preheat the oven to 200°C/400°F/gas mark 6.

Place the turkey in a large stockpot and cover with 3 litres/5 pints of water. Place over a high heat and bring the water to the boil. Skim any scum from the top of the water, reduce the heat to a simmer and leave to cook for 1 hour 15 minutes, until the turkey is cooked through. Remove the turkey from the stockpot and transfer to a large roasting dish. Place a couple of ladlefuls of the cooking water in the base of a large roasting dish and place the turkey on top, breast-side up. Set the rest of the turkey stock aside to cool. Transfer the turkey to the preheated oven and cook, basting occasionally, for around 45 minutes until golden. Check that it is cooked through and continue roasting if needed. Remove from the oven and set aside to cool.

Once the turkey stock has completely cooled, a layer of solidified fat should have formed over the top. Remove the fat from the stock and place in a separate bowl. Set the stock and the fat aside.

Place the walnuts in a food processor and process to a very fine paste. The paste should be sticky and smooth, but not at all grainy (this can take up to 5 minutes). Crush the garlic with the back of a knife and then put in a mortar with a pinch of sea salt. Grind with a pestle to a smooth paste. Place the walnut and garlic pastes in a large bowl with the ground coriander, marigold and fenugreek. Add 2 tablespoons of the reserved turkey stock to the bowl and use your hands to bring the mixture together to a smooth paste. Gradually add enough of the remaining turkey stock to the bowl. Stir to dissolve the walnut paste in the liquid to the consistency of single (light) cream. Set aside.

(continues...)

Place the reserved turkey fat in a large pan over a medium heat. Once hot, add the onions and cook, stirring continuously, until just turning golden. Pour the walnut sauce over the onions and bring to a simmer. Cook, stirring occasionally, for 5 minutes, then add the cinnamon and cloves to the pan and stir to combine. Cook for 10 minutes more.

Crack the eggs into a small bowl with the vinegar and whisk to combine. Pour the eggs into the pan with the sauce and leave until they have coloured and are starting to bubble. Stir to break up the eggs and mix throughout the sauce. Cook for 10 minutes more, season to taste and set aside to cool slightly.

Carve the turkey into large chunks and place the meat in a large serving bowl or platter. Pour the sauce over the turkey and set aside until completely cool. In Georgia, this is traditionally served once a layer of jelly has formed on top.

Katami Sokoti

-CHICKEN WITH MUSHROOMS-

Preparation time: 15 minutes
Cooking time: 50 minutes
Serves 6

1 kg/2 lb 3 oz skinless, boneless
    chicken breasts (approximately
    6 large breasts)
150 ml/5 fl oz/generous ½ cup
    vegetable or sunflower oil
4 large onions, halved and finely sliced
500 g/1 lb 2 oz button mushrooms,
    stalks removed and finely diced
6 garlic cloves
3 tsp ground coriander
5 tsp dried summer savory
1½ tsp ground marigold
40 g/1½ oz unsalted butter
½ tsp hot chilli powder, or to taste
sea salt, to taste
seeds of 1 pomegranate, to garnish
rice or mashed potatoes, to serve

Mushrooms are full of flavour and added bulk and protein to dishes at times when meat was in short supply. This is a rich and comforting dish that is lifted by the addition of jewel-like pomegranate seeds that add sparks of colour and sweetness.

Bring a large pan of water to the boil over a medium heat and add the whole chicken breasts. Cook for around 15 minutes, until cooked through, then drain and set aside to cool.

Place the oil in a large pan over a medium heat. Once hot, add the onions and cook, stirring continuously, until soft and just starting to turn golden, about 10 minutes. Add the mushrooms to the pan and continue to cook, stirring occasionally, until all of the water released from the mushrooms has evaporated, about 10 minutes.

Meanwhile, shred the cooled chicken into long strips with your hands and set aside.

Crush the garlic with the back of a knife and then put in a mortar with a pinch of sea salt. Grind with a pestle to a smooth paste.

When the mushrooms are ready, add the ground coriander, summer savory and marigold and stir to combine. Add the chicken and garlic paste to the pan, stir to combine, and cook, stirring occasionally, for 10–15 minutes to allow the flavours to develop. If the mixture seems too dry, add a little more oil. Season to taste with sea salt.

Divide the mixture between serving plates and scatter over pomegranate seeds. Serve hot with rice or mashed potatoes.

Katmis Kharcho Nigvzis Gareshe

-CHICKEN WITHOUT WALNUTS-

Preparation time: 20 minutes
Cooking time: 1 hour 40 minutes
Serves 4–6

1 medium chicken (approximately
    1–1.2 kg/2 lb 3 oz–2 lb 10 oz)
100 ml/3 ½ fl oz vegetable or sunflower
    oil
5 onions, halved and finely sliced
400 ml/14 fl oz/scant 2 cups crème
    fraîche or sour cream
125 ml/4 fl oz/½ cup whole milk
1 x 400-g/14-oz can chopped tomatoes
1 tsp ground marigold
1 tsp ground blue fenugreek
1 tsp ground coriander
3 garlic cloves, crushed
1 large bunch fresh coriander
    (cilantro), leaves chopped
sea salt and chilli powder, to taste
fresh bread, plain boiled rice or *Gomi*
    (Rice Pudding, see page 93), to serve

If you're cooking a lot of dishes from this book at one time, you may be overwhelmed by the amount of walnuts you seem to be using, so this is a good option for a little reprieve. This chicken stew uses the traditional spice mix (*kharcho suneli*) found in a **kharcho**, but it uses crème fraîche or sour cream as a base rather than walnuts. The result is a lighter dish that still retains the depth of flavour of the traditional version.

Place the chicken in a large stockpot and pour over cold water to completely cover. Place over a high heat and bring to the boil, then reduce the heat to a simmer and leave to cook, covered, until the chicken is completely cooked through, about 45 minutes.

Once the chicken is cooked, transfer to a chopping board and set aside until cool enough to handle. Once cooled, remove and discard the skin and strip all the meat from the bones. Shred the meat with your hands and set aside until needed. You can save the broth that the chicken was cooked in to use in another recipe if you like.

Place the oil in a large pan over a medium heat. Once hot, add the onions and cook, stirring continuously, until soft and just starting to turn golden, about 10 minutes. Add the shredded chicken to the pan, stir to combine and continue to cook, stirring, for 5 minutes.

Meanwhile, place the crème fraîche or sour cream in a small bowl with the milk and stir to combine. Stirring the pan all the time, pour the sauce mixture over the chicken and onions followed by the chopped tomatoes. Add the marigold, fenugreek and ground coriander to the pan and stir to combine. Taste the sauce to check the level of spicing and adjust if necessary. Reduce the heat to a gentle simmer and leave to cook, stirring occasionally, for 30 minutes.

Add the garlic and fresh coriander (cilantro) to the pan and stir to incorporate. Season to taste with sea salt and chilli powder and serve with fresh bread, plain boiled rice or *Gomi*.

Chkmeruli

-POUSSIN IN GARLIC AND WALNUT SAUCE-

Preparation time: 20 minutes, plus at
    least 2 hours' marinating time
Cooking time: 25 minutes
Serves 1

For the poussin:
5 tbsp sunflower or olive oil
½ tsp chilli powder
½ tsp salt
½ tsp paprika
1 corn-fed poussin (approximately
    300 g/10½ oz), spatchcocked

For the sauce:
50 g/1¾ oz/scant ½ cup chopped
    walnuts
3 garlic cloves, crushed
1 tsp sea salt flakes
250 ml/9 fl oz/generous 1 cup boiled
    and cooled water

To serve:
fresh bread

This is an impressive main course that is packed with flavour. The walnuts give the sauce a rich texture and flavour that is enhanced by the fiery raw garlic and the juices from the cooked meat — so make sure you have lots of fresh bread on hand to mop it up. The ingredients given here are for a single serving, but scale it up to suit the number of guests you have.

The poussin can be prepared up to a day ahead. In a small bowl, combine the oil, chilli powder, salt and paprika and mix well to combine. Place the poussin in a shallow dish and pour over the oil and spice mixture to coat. Cover the poussin and transfer to the fridge to marinade for at least 2 hours or overnight.

Preheat the oven to 240°C/475°F/gas mark 9 and line a baking sheet with foil.

Place the marinated poussin and its juices on the baking sheet and transfer to the preheated oven to cook for 20 minutes.

Meanwhile, make the walnut sauce. Place the walnuts in a food processor and process on a high speed until you have a smooth, wet paste. Transfer the walnut paste to a small bowl and set aside.

Put the crushed garlic cloves and salt in a mortar and grind with a pestle until you have a very smooth consistency. Add the garlic to the walnut paste and use your hands to combine.

Now, gradually add the water to the garlic and walnut paste, dissolving the paste in the water each time you add a little more. Keep adding water until the sauce is a thickness you are happy with — you are looking for it to just coat the back of a spoon. Season to taste.

Once the poussin is cooked, remove it from the oven and pour any cooking juices into the walnut sauce, stirring to combine.

Place the poussin on a chopping board and divide into halves or quarters, then transfer to a serving plate. Pour over the walnut and garlic sauce and serve immediately with fresh bread alongside for mopping up the sauce.

Chakhokhbili

-CHICKEN STEW WITH CINNAMON-

Preparation time: 15 minutes
Cooking time: 1 hour 15 minutes
Serves 4–6

1 medium chicken (approximately
    1–1.2 kg/2 lb 3 oz–2 lb 10 oz)
150 ml/5 fl oz/generous ½ cup
    vegetable or sunflower oil
4 large onions, halved and finely sliced
1 tbsp tomato purée (paste)
1 tsp brown sugar
3 x 400-g/14-oz cans chopped
    tomatoes
1 tsp ground cinnamon
½ tsp ground cloves
4 garlic cloves
1 tbsp apple cider vinegar or white
    wine vinegar
1 large handful fresh coriander
    (cilantro), leaves chopped,
    to garnish
sea salt and chilli powder, to taste

Cinnamon can be divisive, but many find it wonderfully warming and fragrant. Here it is used to flavour the sauce of a comforting chicken stew, which is very popular in Georgia, and in my restaurant, during the winter months.

Place the chicken in a large stockpot and pour over cold water to completely cover. Place over a high heat and bring to the boil, then reduce the heat to a simmer and leave to cook, covered, until the chicken is completely cooked through, about 45 minutes.

Once the chicken is cooked, transfer to a chopping board and set aside until cool enough to handle. Once cooled, remove and discard the skin and strip all of the meat from the bones. Shred the meat with your hands and set aside until needed.

Place the oil in a large pan over a medium heat. Once hot, add the onions and cook, stirring continuously, until soft and just starting to turn golden, about 10 minutes. Using a wooden spoon or spatula, push the onions to one side of the pan and add the tomato purée (paste) to the centre of the pan. Cook, stirring continuously, until thickened, about 3 minutes, then combine with the onions.

Add the chopped tomatoes to the pan and stir to combine. Bring to a gentle simmer, then stir in the cinnamon and cloves. Add the chicken to the pan and stir to combine. Leave to cook for 10 minutes for the flavours to develop.

Crush the garlic with the back of a knife and then put in a mortar with a pinch of sea salt. Grind with a pestle to a smooth paste.

Add the garlic to the pan with the chicken and tomato mixture and stir to combine. Cook for another 5 minutes, adding a splash of water if the mixture seems too thick or starts to stick to the base of the pan.

Stir the vinegar through the mixture and season to taste with sea salt and chilli powder. Transfer to serving plates and garnish with the coriander (cilantro). Serve hot.

Sazapkhulo Chakhokhbili

-SUMMER CHICKEN STEW-

Preparation time: 15 minutes
Cooking time: 1 hour 15 minutes
Serves 4–6

1 medium chicken (approximately
    1–1.2 kg/2 lb 3 oz–2 lb 10 oz)
1 kg/2 lb 3 oz fresh tomatoes
150 ml/5 fl oz/generous ½ cup
    vegetable or sunflower oil
4 large onions, halved and finely sliced
4 garlic cloves
1 bunch fresh coriander (cilantro),
    leaves chopped
1 bunch fresh dill, chopped
1 bunch fresh parsley, leaves chopped
1 bunch fresh pink basil, leaves torn

This can be seen as the summer alternative to the recipe on the previous page. Whereas that one is heavy with spice, this one is lifted with fresh tomatoes and a medley of beautifully fragrant fresh herbs for a much lighter dish, packed with the fresh and vibrant flavours of the season.

Place the chicken in a large stockpot and pour over cold water to completely cover. Place over a high heat and bring to the boil, then reduce the heat to a simmer and leave to cook, covered, until the chicken is completely cooked through, about 45 minutes.

Meanwhile, prepare the tomatoes by scoring a shallow cross at the base of each and placing in a large bowl. Pour over boiling water to cover, then leave for a few seconds until you see the skins start to split and peel away around the cross. Drain the tomatoes and submerge immediately in cold water. Peel off and discard the skins and place the skinned tomatoes in a large bowl. Using your hands, pulp the skinned tomatoes to extract all of their juice and set aside until needed.

Once the chicken is cooked, transfer to a chopping board and set aside until cool enough to handle. Once cooled, remove and discard the skin and strip all of the meat from the bones. Shred the meat with your hands and set aside until needed.

Place the oil in a large pan over a medium heat. Once hot, add the onions and cook, stirring continuously, until soft and just starting to turn golden, about 10 minutes. Add the shredded chicken and pulped tomatoes to the pan with the onions and stir to combine. Bring to a gentle simmer and cook, stirring occasionally, for 15 minutes.

Crush the garlic with the back of a knife and then put in a mortar with a pinch of sea salt. Grind with a pestle to a smooth paste.

Add the garlic paste and all of the fresh herbs to the pan and stir to combine. Cook for 5 minutes to allow the flavours to develop, then season to taste.

Transfer to a serving dish and serve hot.

Kalia

-LAYERED CHICKEN-

Preparation time: 40 minutes,
  plus at least 3 hours' marinating
  time
Cooking time: 2 hours
Serves 6

1 medium chicken or 1 kg/2 lb 3 oz
  skin–on jointed chicken pieces (a
  mixture of breast, drumsticks and
  thighs is ideal)
7 large onions, halved and finely sliced
1 tsp vegetable or sunflower oil
50 g/1¾ oz unsalted butter, melted
seeds of 2 large pomegranates
1 tsp ground marigold
1 tsp ground blue fenugreek
1 tsp ground coriander
1 tsp dried summer savory
1 head of garlic (optional)
sea salt and freshly ground black
  pepper
1 handful fresh coriander (cilantro),
  leaves chopped, to garnish

This wonderful dish is prepared and cooked in one pot and, once assembled, can be left bubbling on the stovetop without so much as a second thought, making it the perfect option for when you have people coming over and would rather be entertaining than in the kitchen. The wonderfully vibrant pomegranate seeds lose their colour during cooking, but melt down to form a rich sweet and sour sauce that coats the deliciously tender chicken pieces.

If you are using a whole chicken, use a sharp knife to cut along the joints and separate the meat into portions of breast, drumstick and thigh. You can retain the rest of the carcass for making stock. Set aside.

Layer half the onions in the base of a large stockpot or stovetop-proof casserole dish. Drizzle over the oil and half of the melted butter. Season, then layer half the chicken pieces on top of the onions, seasoning again and then topping with half of the pomegranate seeds. Mix the marigold, fenugreek and ground coriander together to make up a *kharcho suneli* spice mix and sprinkle half of it over the pomegranate, then repeat the layers, continuing to season between each layer, ending with a final sprinkling of the spice mix. Sprinkle the dried summer savory over the top, then cover the pan and transfer to the fridge for 3–4 hours to allow the flavours to settle and develop.

When you are ready to cook, remove the dish from the fridge and place over a low heat. Sit the whole head of garlic, if using, on top of the layered chicken and place the lid back on the pan. Cook for 2 hours, until the chicken is cooked and deliciously moist.

Take the lid off the pan and squeeze the garlic cloves (if using) from their skins into the pan. Scatter over fresh coriander (cilantro) and place the dish in the middle of the table for everyone to dig in.

Katmis Gvidzli

-CHICKEN LIVERS-

Preparation time: 15 minutes,
    plus 30 minutes' soaking time
Cooking time: 40 minutes
Serves 4–6

1 kg/2 lb 3 oz chicken livers
whole milk, for soaking
200 ml/7 fl oz/generous ¾ cup
    vegetable or sunflower oil
½ tsp hot chilli powder, or to taste
4 large onions, cut in half and finely
    sliced
325 ml/11 fl oz/generous 1¼ cups dry
    white wine
4 tbsp pomegranate molasses
3 tbsp ground coriander
4 tsp dried summer savory
4 garlic cloves
sea salt and freshly ground black
    pepper
1 large handful fresh coriander
    (cilantro), leaves chopped, to
    garnish
seeds of 1 pomegranate, to garnish

This is one of my favourite ways to start a meal. The delicious richness of chicken livers is cut through by the sour punch of pomegranate molasses. It's easy to overcook chicken livers, but soaking them in milk first will ensure that they remain tender and unctuous.

Place the chicken livers in a large bowl and pour over enough milk to completely cover. Set aside to soak in the milk for 30 minutes — this ensures the meat is tender after cooking.

Preheat the oven to 220°C/425°F/gas mark 7.

Drain the chicken livers, then rinse under the hot tap (faucet), followed straight away by the cold tap — this helps to ensure that the texture of the meat is nice and tight before cooking. Lay the livers on a large baking sheet and drizzle over 50 ml/2 fl oz of the oil, using your hands to ensure the livers are well coated. Season with salt, pepper and chilli powder and transfer to the preheated oven to cook for 20 minutes, turning the livers over halfway through cooking.

Meanwhile, place the remaining 150 ml/5 fl oz/generous ½ cup of oil in a large pan over a medium heat. Once hot, add the onions and cook, stirring continuously, until soft and just starting to turn golden, about 10 minutes. Add the wine to the pan and continue to cook over a gentle heat, stirring occasionally, until all the alcohol has dissolved, about 10 minutes.

Add the pomegranate molasses to the pan and stir to combine. Cook for 5 minutes more, stirring occasionally, then add the ground coriander and summer savory to the pan and stir to combine.

Crush the garlic with the back of a knife and then put in a mortar with a pinch of sea salt. Grind with a pestle to a smooth paste.

Remove the livers from the oven and add to the pan along with any juices and the garlic. Stir to combine and season to taste.

Transfer the mixture to a serving platter and garnish with fresh coriander (cilantro) and pomegranate seeds. Serve hot.

Tabaka

-SPICED PAN-FRIED POUSSIN-

Preparation time: 10 minutes,
    plus 2 hours for soaking and
    marinating
Cooking time: 25 minutes
Serves 1

1 corn-fed poussin (approximately
    300 g/10½ oz), spatchcocked
1 tbsp apple cider vinegar or white
    wine vinegar
3 garlic cloves
1 tsp ground coriander
½ tsp sea salt
1 tsp ground blue fenugreek
4 tbsp vegetable or sunflower oil
¼ tsp red chilli powder
¼ tsp paprika
new potatoes and *Tkemali* (Plum
    Sauce, see page 22), to serve

The secret of this eternally popular dish is to get the poussin as flat as possible in the pan and apply weight to the top of the bird during cooking to ensure maximum contact with the heat. This will result in a deliciously crisp skin that gives way to tender and juicy meat.

Place the poussin in a snug-fitting bowl.

Place the garlic and the vinegar in a mortar and grind with a pestle to a smooth paste, adding a dash of water if the mixture is too dry. Add the ground coriander, salt, blue fenugreek, oil, chilli powder and paprika to this mixture and stir to combine.

Pour the spice mixture over the poussin, using your hands to ensure that the poussin is well coated. Cover and transfer to the fridge for at least 1 hour, but ideally overnight.

When you are ready to cook the poussin, place a large frying pan (skillet) over a medium heat. Once hot, lay the poussin in the pan breast-side down, then lay a pan lid or plate over the top and weigh it down with something heavy (tins from your kitchen cupboard work well). Cook the poussin until the base is golden, around 10 minutes. Remove the pan lid or plate, then flip the poussin in the pan and cook for another 10 minutes until golden and cooked through.

Serve hot with new potatoes and *Tkemali*.

Tabaka

Late Summer, spiced pan-fried poussin with my great uncle in a village in western Georgia

At the end of summer, I would often go to stay with my grandfather's brother in his village in western Georgia. I was very little and I loved spending time there. My great uncle used to wake me up when it was sunrise and I would run barefoot through the dewy grass. Outside there was a big pot of water that the sun gradually warmed, making it hot enough to bathe in.

My special place was a big tree that was over 100 years old; there was a swing for me on a branch and a bird's nest on a bough. An old man called Vene lived with my family in a little house in their garden and I loved the stories he told me. I used to go to his house in the morning and wake him up. His house smelled of corn sacks and wood smoke, and there were chickens scratching around and little mice hiding in the nooks and crannies. He passed away when I was four years old and it was the first time that I experienced the sadness of death. Before lunch he used to have a little nap underneath

my tree and I remember wondering how many people had shared their secrets with the tree. After lunch every day, my aunt and I picked blackberries while *tabaka* roasted in the fireplace. We would then prepare walnut or blackberry sauce to serve with it. The poussin had deliciously crisp skin, but the flesh was tender and moist. Although we ate it every day, I never once grew tired of it.

I also used to visit during the wine harvest in early autumn. I remember one evening where I walked in the vineyard with Vene. It was a beautiful night and the vineyard looked magical. He held freshly picked grapes and they seemed to float in his palm. I remember the amber colour playing against drops of falling rain so that it looked like they were weeping. He said to me in the softest of voices, 'Look at the grapes. They look like beautiful women, you look at them and are captivated. It's like a magic potion, one sip and you are forever in love'.

Fish Dishes

-CHAPTER 7-

Tevzi Kindzmarshi

-SALMON WITH GARLIC AND CORIANDER SAUCE-

Preparation time: 10 minutes
Cooking time: 10 minutes
Serves 2

1 onion, halved
3 allspice berries
3 bay leaves
2 salmon fillets (approximately
   250 g/9 oz each)
4 garlic cloves
2 fresh coriander (cilantro) sprigs,
   roughly chopped
2 fresh dill sprigs, roughly chopped
1 tsp salt
1 tbsp apple cider vinegar or white
   wine vinegar, or to taste
1 fresh green chilli, finely chopped,
   or to taste

Salmon has deliciously soft flesh that is packed with healthy fats. Here a pungent sauce of pounded coriander (cilantro), dill and fiery raw garlic are paired with the fish to cut through the richness. This is a wonderfully simple way to make a flavour-packed sauce, which you could pair with any kind of fish or simple grilled (broiled) meat.

Place 1 litre/1 ¾ pints/4 cups boiling water in a large pan over a medium heat. Add the halved onion, allspice berries, and bay leaves to the pan and bring to the boil. Reduce the heat to a simmer and add the salmon. Cook for 5 minutes, then lift the salmon fillets out of the pan and set aside. Drain the broth through a colander and retain half of it.

Put the garlic, fresh herbs and salt in a mortar and grind to a paste with a pestle. Transfer the paste to a bowl and loosen with a couple of spoonfuls of the reserved stock, until you're happy with the consistency. Add vinegar and fresh chilli to taste.

Place the cooked salmon fillets on serving plates and pour over the garlic and coriander sauce. Allow to cool and serve.

Kalmakhi

-BAKED TROUT WITH BASIL AND LEMON-

Preparation time: 10 minutes
Cooking time: 30 minutes
Serves 1

1 ½ tbsp vegetable or sunflower oil
1 onion, finely chopped
¼ tsp granulated sugar
1 whole trout, scaled, gutted and
  cleaned
2 lemon slices
1 tsp dried basil
sea salt and freshly ground black
  pepper
Akhali Kartophili (New Potatoes with
  Chilli and Herbs, see page 50) and
  Tkemali (Plum Sauce, see page 22),
  to serve

Fish isn't widely eaten in Georgia, but when it is, preparations tend to be simple to allow the delicate flavours to speak for themselves. Here, a whole trout is stuffed simply with basil and lemon and cooked *en papillote* for a quick, healthy and undeniably delicious supper.

Preheat the oven to 200°C/400°F/gas mark 6 and lightly oil a large sheet of parchment paper.

Place the oil in a large frying pan (skillet) over a medium heat. Once hot, add the onions and cook stirring continuously, until soft and just golden, about 10 minutes. Add the sugar to the pan, stir to combine and set the pan aside to cool.

Once the onions have cooled slightly, use them to stuff the trout. Top the onions with the lemon slices and sprinkle over the basil.

Place the trout in the centre of the parchment paper and fold in the edges to enclose the trout and form a parcel. Transfer to a baking sheet and place in the preheated oven for 10 minutes, until the eyes of the fish are opaque, then open the parcel and return the trout to the oven for 2 minutes to allow the skin to crisp up.

Transfer to a serving plate and serve with *Akhali Kartophili* and *Tkemali*.

Kalmakhi Sunelebit

-TROUT WITH GEORGIAN SPICES-

Preparation time: 10 minutes
Cooking time: 15 minutes
Serves 1

vegetable or sunflower oil, for greasing
½ garlic clove, crushed
2 tbsp sour cream
½ tsp ground coriander
½ tsp ground blue fenugreek
½ tsp ground marigold
1 whole trout, gutted, cleaned and
    scaled
seeds of ½ pomegranate
1 coriander (cilantro) sprig, leaves
    picked, to garnish
2 lemon slices
sea salt and chilli powder, to taste

The traditional Georgian flavours of ground coriander, fenugreek and marigold are combined with sour cream to create a mellow but flavoursome coating for delicate baked trout. Pomegranate seeds, coriander (cilantro) and lemon wedges are used to finish the dish and provide notes of sweet and sour that beautifully balance and allow the delicate flavour of the fish to shine.

Preheat the oven to 200°C/400°F/gas mark 6 and lightly oil a large sheet of parchment paper.

Place the garlic, sour cream, coriander, fenugreek and marigold in a bowl and stir to combine. Set aside for 5 minutes to allow the flavours to develop.

Coat the trout with the sauce inside and out, then place in the centre of the parchment paper and fold in the edges to enclose the trout and form a parcel. Transfer to a baking sheet and place in the preheated oven for 10 minutes, until the eyes of the fish are opaque.

Transfer to a serving plate and scatter over the pomegranate seeds. Season to taste with sea salt and chilli powder. Serve the trout hot, garnished with coriander (cilantro) leaves and with lemon wedges on the side for squeezing.

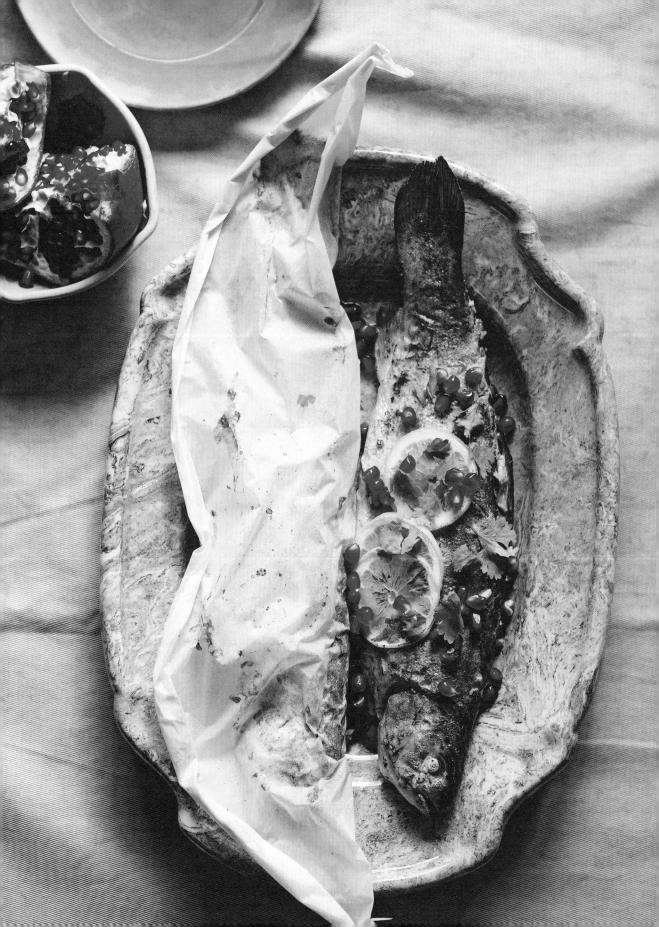

Tevzis Mtsvadi

-FISH KEBABS-

Preparation time: 10 minutes, plus at
  least 2 hours' marinating time
Cooking time: 10 minutes
Serves 6

1 kg/2 lb 3 oz mixed fish and shellfish
  (salmon, tuna, king prawns [jumbo
  shrimp])
2 onions, halved and finely sliced
1½ tbsp mayonnaise
1 tsp *Mshrali Ajika* (Dry Red Chilli
  Paste, see page 29)
plain boiled rice, to serve

wooden or metal skewers

These kebabs are a great way of using up any fish that you have in the fridge, and they make a lovely addition to the table at any summer meal or barbecue. The marinade can be made ahead and the fish left in the fridge overnight to allow the flavours to develop, but, whether prepared in the oven or on the barbecue, the cooking time is minimal.

Place the fish, shellfish and onions in a large bowl and mix to combine. In another bowl, mix the *Ajika* and mayonnaise to combine, then pour over the fish and onion mixture, using your hands to ensure everything is well coated. Transfer to the fridge, covered, for at least 2 hours or overnight to let the flavours develop.

Half an hour before you want to cook the kebabs, preheat the oven to 200°C/400°F/gas mark 6 and line a large baking sheet with foil. If using wooden skewers, soak them in water or oil to prevent them from burning in the oven.

Thread the fish onto the skewers, ensuring that you have a good mix of fish on each skewer. Lay the skewers on the prepared baking sheet and top with the onions. Season with salt and pepper and transfer to the preheated oven to cook for 10 minutes, until the fish is cooked through and the onions are just soft, but still retaining some bite.

Serve the skewers warm with plain boiled rice as a side.

Tevzi Maionezis Sausit

-CRISPY FISH IN SPICED MAYONNAISE AND WALNUT SAUCE-

Preparation time: 20 minutes
Cooking time: 8 minutes
Serves 4

1 kg/2 lb 3 oz white fish fillets (cod, haddock or pollock all work well)
4 eggs, beaten, in a bowl
200 g/7 oz panko breadcrumbs, in a bowl
100 ml/3½ fl oz vegetable or sunflower oil
sea salt and freshly ground black pepper

For the sauce:
100 g/3½ oz/¾ cup chopped walnuts
3 garlic cloves
1 tsp ground coriander
1 tsp ground blue fenugreek
1 tsp ground marigold
¼ tsp red chilli powder, or to taste
200 g/7 oz mayonnaise

These are essentially a Georgian take on fish fingers. Delicate white fish is fried in breadcrumbs and served with a deliciously spicy walnut and mayonnaise sauce. As well as making a wonderful dish for the dinner table, these could be adapted to make flavoursome canapés.

Place the walnuts in a food processor and process to a very fine paste. The paste should be sticky and smooth, but not at all grainy (this can take up to 5 minutes).

Crush the garlic with the back of a knife and then put in a mortar with a pinch of the sea salt. Grind with a pestle to a smooth paste and set aside.

Place the walnut and garlic pastes in a bowl with the ground coriander, fenugreek, marigold and chilli powder. Add 100 ml/3½ fl oz of water and use your hands to bring the mixture together to form a smooth sauce. Transfer the sauce to a blender along with the mayonnaise and blend until smooth. Season to taste and set aside.

Put the bowl of beaten eggs and the bowl of breadcrumbs on a work surface. Then, working with one piece of fish at a time, dip the fish fillets into the egg and then roll in the breadcrumbs. Transfer to a plate while you finish the rest of the fish. Once you have breaded all of the fish, repeat the process so that all of the fillets have a double coating of breadcrumbs.

Heat the oil in a large frying pan (skillet) over a medium heat. Once hot, add the fish to the pan and cook one side until golden and crispy, around 4 minutes. Carefully flip the fish and cook on the reverse side for another 4 minutes.

Serve the fish hot with the mayonnaise sauce drizzled over.

Tevzi Maionezis Sausit

The smell of crispy fish in spiced mayonnaise and walnut sauce

Throughout her life my mother was never fond of fish. If anyone was cooking fish at home, she had to leave the house for the day because she could not bear the smell. By contrast, my father, grandmother and I all loved fish and any time that my mother left the house, we took the oppotunity to cook some. On one Saturday each month my mother would visit her mother for the day, and the moment she left would signify the start of great activity in the kitchen. My grandmother would dip fish in breadcrumbs, fry it until deliciously crispy and serve it with a creamy mayonnaise and walnut sauce. My father, grandmother and I would all huddle together in the kitchen, eating it guiltily and revelling in our shared secret, always with one eye on the clock to watch for when my mother would return. As soon as we had finished eating, we would throw open all the doors and windows of the house in an attempt to banish the smell and keep my mother from discovering our secret. Sometimes it even worked.

Oraguli Masharapit

-BAKED SALMON WITH POMEGRANATE MOLASSES-

Preparation time: 20 minutes,
 plus marinating time
Cooking time: 20 minutes
Serves 4

1 kg/2 lb 3 oz skin-on salmon fillet, cut
 into bite-sized chunks
4 onions, finely sliced
1 lemon, finely sliced
1 tbsp vegetable or sunflower oil,
 plus extra for greasing
pomegranate molasses, to serve
sea salt, to taste

wooden or metal skewers, lightly oiled

This simply prepared dish of baked salmon and onions is served with mouth-puckeringly sour pomegranate molasses to cut through the richness of the salmon.

The day before you want to serve the dish, place the salmon in a large baking dish with the onion and lemon slices. Season generously with sea salt and toss together with your hands to ensure everything is well combined. Cover with clingfilm (plastic wrap) and transfer to the fridge overnight to allow the flavours to develop.

Half an hour before you want to cook the salmon, preheat the oven to 200°C/400°F/gas mark 6 and line a large baking sheet with parchment paper.

Remove the mixture from the fridge, discard the lemon pieces and reserve the onions to use later. Push the salmon pieces onto the prepared skewers, place them on the prepared baking sheet and season generously. Transfer to the preheated oven for 8 minutes, then scatter over the reserved onions and drizzle over the oil. Return to the oven for another 8 minutes, until the fish is cooked through and the onions are soft.

Transfer to serving plates and drizzle over pomegranate molasses to serve.

Vegetable Dishes

-CHAPTER 8-

Kotnis Lobio

-FRAGRANT ROSE COCO BEANS-

Preparation time: 20 minutes,
  plus at least 3 hours' soaking time
Cooking time: 1 hour 30 minutes
Serves 4–6 as part of a *supra*

1 kg/2 lb 3 oz dried rose coco or
  borlotti (cranberry) beans
1 leek, finely chopped
20 g/¾ oz celery, finely chopped
1 green chilli, finely chopped
6 onions, finely chopped
3 tbsp vegetable or sunflower oil
5 garlic cloves, crushed
2 sweet pointed peppers, finely
  chopped
20 g/¾ oz fresh dill, chopped
30 g/¾ oz fresh parsley leaves,
  chopped
30 g/¾ oz fresh coriander (cilantro)
  leaves, chopped
sea salt and freshly ground black
  pepper
fresh bread and pickled vegetables,
  to serve

In times of scarcity, *lobio* (dried beans) were the saviour of the Georgian people. Nutritious and packed with protein, they added bulk to any meal at times when meat was hard to come by.

Place the beans in a large bowl and cover with cold water. Set aside to soak for 3–4 hours or overnight, until swollen. Drain and rinse.

Place the soaked beans in a large pan with enough water to cover. Place over a medium heat and bring to the boil, then immediately drain and rinse the beans and return to the pan with a fresh batch of water. Bring to the boil again and cook for around 1 hour, until tender, adding more water during the cooking process if necessary.

Once the beans are tender, add the leek, celery, chilli and half of the onions to the pan and stir to combine. Leave to cook for 10 minutes, stirring occasionally.

Place the oil in a separate large pan over a medium heat. Once hot, add the remaining onions, the peppers and garlic and cook, stirring continuously, until soft and translucent, about 10 minutes. Add the cooked onions, peppers and garlic to the pan with the beans and stir to combine, adding a little more water if the mixture is too thick.

Cook the mixture for 5 minutes more, then stir through the chopped herbs and season to taste. Serve hot with fresh bread and pickled vegetables.

Ajabsandali

-AUBERGINE STEW-

Preparation time: 10 minutes
Cooking time: 25 minutes
Serves 6

150 ml/5 fl oz/generous ½ cup
   vegetable or sunflower oil
4 onions, halved and finely sliced
4 garlic cloves, crushed
1 red bird's eye chilli, chopped,
   or to taste
1 kg/2 lb 3 oz aubergines (eggplants),
   peeled and chopped into bite-sized
   chunks
3 long red peppers, finely sliced
1 tbsp tomato purée (paste)
1 x 400-g/14-oz can chopped tomatoes
1 handful fresh pink basil or 10 g/
   5 tbsp dried green or pink basil,
   chopped
1 handful fresh parsley, chopped
1 handful fresh coriander (cilantro),
   chopped

For me, this dish is the taste of summer and instantly recalls the seemingly never-ending summers spent with my family during my school holidays. Fragrant with fresh herbs and deliciously soft aubergines (eggplants), you can make a big pot of this ahead of time and enjoy it over a few days as the flavours meld and develop.

Heat the oil in a large pan over a medium heat. Once hot, add the onions, half the garlic and the chilli and cook, stirring continuously, until soft and translucent, about 10 minutes. Add the aubergines (eggplants) and red peppers and continue to cook, stirring, for around 10 minutes, until soft and tender.

Using a wooden spoon or spatula, push the vegetables to the side of the pan. Add the tomato purée (paste) to the centre of the pan and cook, stirring, for around 2 minutes, until thickened, then incorporate with the other vegetables.

Add the chopped tomatoes, fresh herbs and the remaining garlic to the pan and cook, stirring, for another 3 minutes to allow the flavours to develop. Season to taste and serve hot.

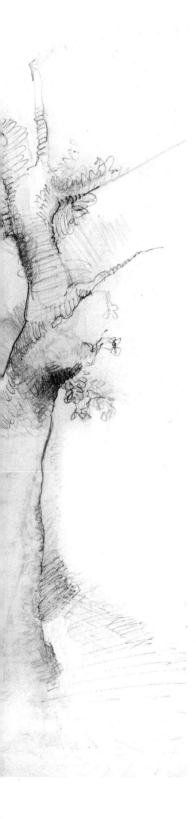

Ajabsandali

Aubergine stew, my favourite Summer food

The smell of *ajabsandali* instantly recalls a moment in my youth when I was returning home to Tbilisi at the end of August from a long summer holiday away. The city is very humid and the air smells of hot pavements as we drive through the streets towards home. The whole city feels empty and sad, but upon opening the door to my house, I am immediately met with the fragrant and unmistakable smell of *ajabsandali*: basil, aubergines (eggplants) and something fresh. My grandmother rushes to greet me at the door. She is flushed and exhausted by the heat, but the twinkle in her eye tells me that she has a surprise for me. I soon found out what it is; our dining table is groaning under the weight of a feast of all of my favourite dishes, prepared to welcome me home. The table is full of fresh herbs, salads of simple cucumber and tomato with pink basil, my favourite cheese and my favourite drinks, and at the centre of it all is *ajabsandali*. I tell my granny about the summer holidays and everything in the house is quiet and calm. I am home.

Soko Ketze

-MUSHROOMS BAKED WITH CHEESE-

Preparation time: 5 minutes
Cooking time: 10–15 minutes
Serves 1–2

7–8 field mushrooms, stalks removed
50 g/1¾ oz butter, softened – you
    could mix this with ½ tsp *Ajika*
    (chilli paste, see pages 29–31) for a
    spiced butter
50 g/1¾ oz grated mozzarella cheese
freshly chopped dill, to serve
sea salt and freshly ground black
    pepper, to taste

This is my go-to meal for those days when I don't have the energy to cook, but want something comforting, warm and delicious. Wonderfully buttery and cheesy, you will find yourself devouring these by the plateful.

Preheat the oven to 200°C/400°F/gas mark 6.

Lay the mushrooms snugly in the base of an ovenproof baking dish. Divide the butter (or spiced butter) between the mushroom cups and season with salt and pepper. Transfer to the preheated oven to bake for 5–8 minutes, until tender.

Remove from the oven and scatter over the grated cheese. Return to the oven to bake until the cheese is golden and bubbling. Garnish with fresh dill and serve.

Sokos Shilaplavi

-CREAMY RICE WITH MUSHROOMS-

Preparation time: 10 minutes
Cooking time: 45 minutes
Serves 6

1 kg/2 lb 3 oz chestnut mushrooms,
   quartered
100 ml/3 ½ fl oz vegetable or
   sunflower oil
3 onions, finely chopped
1 tsp ground caraway seeds
1 tsp finely ground black pepper
pinch of sea salt
500 g/1 lb 2 oz short-grain rice

This dish of delicately flavoured rice and mushrooms is traditionally served at funerals, where its simple, warming flavours are supposed to bring comfort and solace to the mourners. Don't be put off by this, as it can easily provide comfort at other times too, and there are times when we all need a bit comfort.

Place the mushrooms in a large pan with 1 cm/½ inch of water and place over a medium heat. Bring to a simmer and cook for 5 minutes, until the mushrooms are tender.

Heat the oil in a large pan over a medium heat. Once hot, add the onions and cook, stirring continuously, for 10 minutes, until soft and translucent. Drain the mushrooms and add to the pan with the onions. Cook for 5 minutes, stirring occasionally, then remove from the heat and set aside.

Place 1.6 litres/3 pints of cold water in a large pan over a high heat. Once simmering, reduce the heat to low and add the ground caraway seeds, black pepper and the salt. Add the rice to the pan, followed by the mushroom and onion mixture. Cover the pan and wrap the lid with a clean tea (dish) towel or muslin (cheesecloth), then leave to cook for 20 minutes, until the rice is cooked through, adding more water to the pan if necessary. Transfer to a serving dish and serve hot.

Soko Sunelebit

-SPICED STUFFED MUSHROOMS-

Preparation time: 10 minutes
Cooking time: 30 minutes
Serves 1

8 closed-cup mushrooms, cups and
    stalks separated
3 tbsp vegetable or sunflower oil
50 g/1¾ oz butter
1 onion, finely chopped
¼ tsp ground coriander
¼ tsp dried summer savory
¼ tsp ground marigold
2 garlic cloves, crushed
50 g/1¾ oz grated mozzarella cheese
1 small bunch fresh coriander
    (cilantro), leaves chopped, to serve
sea salt and chilli powder, to taste

For many vegetarians, a stuffed mushroom is the epitome of lazy dinner-party cooking, but these will be sure to have even the most cynical coming back for more. Rich with the mellow, fragrant flavours of Georgian spices and bubbling with soft, golden cheese, these are the ultimate in Georgian comfort food.

Preheat the oven to 200°C/400°F/gas mark 6.

Lay the mushroom cups snugly in the base of an ovenproof baking dish and set aside. Coarsely chop the mushroom stalks.

Place the oil and butter in a large frying pan (skillet) over a medium heat. Once hot, add the onions and cook, stirring continuously, until soft and translucent, about 10 minutes.

Add the chopped mushroom stalks, ground coriander, summer savory and marigold to the pan and cook, stirring continuously, until the mushroom stalks are tender, about 5 minutes. Add the garlic to the pan and cook, still stirring for another 2 minutes, then remove from the heat.

Spoon the cooked mushroom mixture into the mushroom cups, generously filling each one, then scatter over the grated mozzarella. Transfer to the preheated oven for 10–15 minutes, until the cheese is melted and golden. Scatter over the fresh coriander (cilantro), season to taste with sea salt and chilli powder and serve hot.

Kombostos Ruleti

-CABBAGE ROULADE-

Preparation time: 15 minutes
Cooking time: 15 minutes
Serves 4–6 as part of a *supra*

1 large white cabbage (approximately
    1 kg/2 lb 3 oz)
3 tbsp vegetable or sunflower oil
2 carrots, grated
2 onions, finely chopped
200 g/7 oz/scant 1¾ cups chopped
    walnuts
3 garlic cloves
2 tsp ground coriander
1 tsp ground marigold
1 tsp ground blue fenugreek
3 tbsp apple cider vinegar or white
    wine vinegar
1 large bunch fresh coriander
    (cilantro), leaves chopped
1 small bunch fresh parsley, leaves
    chopped
1 small bunch fresh dill, chopped
pomegranate seeds, to garnish
sea salt and chilli powder, to taste

These delicate spirals of stuffed cabbage look very elegant on the plate and make great canapés as they can be picked up and eaten in a couple of mouthfuls. The filling of carrot and onion adds a sweetness that helps to alleviate the richness of the spiced walnut paste, and it is complemented by an abundance of fragrant fresh herbs.

Using a knife, work around the central core of the cabbage at the base to lightly perforate it. Place the whole cabbage in a large pan and pour over salted boiling water to just cover. Place over a medium heat, bring the water back to the boil and cook for 2–3 minutes, until the leaves have just started to soften and pull away from the body of the cabbage. Drain and set aside to cool.

Heat the oil in a large frying pan (skillet) over a medium heat. Once hot, add the carrots and onions and cook, stirring continuously, until soft but not coloured, about 10 minutes. Set aside to cool.

Place the walnuts in a food processor and process to a very fine paste. The paste should be sticky and smooth, but not at all grainy (this can take up to 5 minutes). Crush the garlic with the back of a knife and then put in a mortar with a pinch of sea salt. Grind with a pestle to a smooth paste.

Place the walnut and garlic pastes in a bowl with the ground coriander, marigold, fenugreek and vinegar. Using your hands, bring the mixture together to a smooth, thick paste. The paste should be a similar texture to a loose hummus, so add a few drops of water if it is too thick. Add the cooked onion and carrot mixture to the bowl along with all the fresh herbs, and stir to ensure everything is well combined. Season to taste with sea salt and chilli powder.

Peel the leaves off the cooled cabbage and lay flat. Using a knife, slice out any particularly woody central stalks from the base of the leaves, being careful to leave the top of the leaves intact.

Working with one leaf at a time, lay the cabbage leaves flat on a chopping board and spread with a generous spoonful of the filling mixture. Starting at a narrow edge, roll the leaves into tight spirals. The leaves can then be transferred to a serving plate as they are or sliced into 2.5-cm/1-inch rounds for more delicate mouthfuls. Scatter over pomegranate seeds to garnish and serve.

Dolma

-STUFFED CABBAGE PARCELS-

Preparation time: 25 minutes
Cooking time: 55 minutes
Serves 6

1 medium white cabbage
150 ml/5 fl oz/generous ½ cup
   vegetable or sunflower oil
1 green chilli
4 carrots, peeled and grated
4 garlic cloves, crushed
freshly ground black pepper
5 onions, finely chopped
185 g/6½ oz/1 cup short-grain rice
1 Granny Smith apple, grated
250 ml/9 fl oz/generous 1 cup sour
   cream or 100 g/3½ oz tomato purée
   (paste)
sea salt and freshly ground black
   pepper
red chilli powder, to taste
sour cream and *Ziteli Ajika* (Red
   Chilli Paste, see page 30), to serve

These stuffed cabbage leaves make a wonderful vegetarian main course to serve at a *supra*. Stuffed with delicately spiced rice and vegetables and served with a rich tomato, or sour cream sauce, and spicy *Ajika*, they are filling, warming and full of flavour.

Using a knife, work around the central core of the cabbage at the base to lightly perforate it. Place the whole cabbage in a large pan and pour over salted boiling water to just cover. Place over a medium heat, bring the water back to the boil and cook for 2–3 minutes, until the leaves have just started to soften and pull away from the body of the cabbage. Drain and set aside to cool.

Heat the oil in a large frying pan (skillet) over a medium heat. Once hot, add the onions, chilli and garlic and cook, stirring continuously, until the onions are soft and translucent, about 10 minutes. Add the carrots to the pan and continue to cook, stirring, for another 5 minutes.

Bring a pan of boiling water to the boil, add the rice and cook until almost tender. Drain, then rinse in cold water and drain again.

Place the rice in a large bowl with the onion and carrot mixture and grated apple and use a fork to combine. Set aside.

Peel the leaves off the cooled cabbage and lay flat. Using a knife, slice out any particularly woody central stalks from the base of the leaves, being careful to leave the top of the leaves intact.

Working with one leaf at a time, place a spoonful of the rice mixture in the centre of each leaf, bring in the sides and roll up to enclose the filling. Place the cabbage rolls in the base of a large pan and set aside.

To make the sauce, dissolve either the sour cream or tomato purée (paste) in 500 ml/18 fl oz/2 cups water and pour over the cabbage leaves. Season to taste with salt, pepper and chilli powder. Place a snug-fitting plate over the top of the cabbage rolls and weigh it down with something heavy (the pestle from a pestle and mortar works well for this). Place the pan over a gentle heat and bring the sauce to a simmer. Leave to cook for 30–40 minutes, until the rice is tender.

Serve the rolls hot with the sauce spooned over the top and sour cream and *Ajika* on the side for dipping.

Chanakhi (Vegetarianuli)

-LAYERED VEGETABLES-

Preparation time: 20 minutes
Cooking time: 1 hour
Serves 6

3 (bell) peppers (mixed colours),
    deseeded, halved and sliced
1–2 bird's eye chillies, chopped, to
    taste
30 g/1 oz fresh coriander (cilantro)
    leaves, chopped
30 g/1 oz fresh parsley leaves, chopped
30 g/1 oz fresh dill, chopped
30 g/1 oz fresh tarragon leaves,
    chopped
30 g/1 oz fresh basil leaves, torn
220 ml/7 ½ fl oz vegetable or sunflower
    oil
700 g/1 lb 9 oz aubergines (eggplants),
    sliced into 1-cm/¼-inch rounds
700 g/1 lb 9 oz medium white
    potatoes, sliced into wedges
2 x 400-g/14-oz cans chopped
    tomatoes
4 onions, halved and finely sliced
7 garlic cloves, crushed
1 tsp butter
sea salt and freshly ground black
    pepper
rice and sour cream, to serve

This dish of layered vegetables can be assembled ahead then left in the fridge until it is ready to cook. This would make a wonderful vegetarian main course but also a great side dish for a large _supra_. If you are making it for vegetarians, be sure to tell any meat eaters to keep their hands off because it will be gone in seconds!

Place the (bell) peppers in a large bowl with the chillies and all the fresh herbs and toss to combine. Set aside.

Pour enough of the oil into a large cast-iron pan to coat the base and reserve the rest for later. Place a layer of aubergines (eggplants) in the base of the pan, followed by a layer of potatoes, then a layer of the pepper and herb mix, a layer of chopped tomatoes and a layer of onions. Repeat the layers until all of the ingredients are used up.

Place the garlic in a bowl with 120 ml/4 fl oz water and stir to combine. Pour this mixture over the layered vegetables followed by the remaining oil. Season generously with salt and pepper and dot the butter over the top.

Cover the pan with a tight-fitting lid and place over a medium heat for 40–60 minutes, until the vegetables are tender. Serve hot with rice and sour cream on the side.

Kartophilis Chashushuli

-SPICED POTATO AND EGG STEW-

Preparation time: 10 minutes
Cooking time: 30 minutes
Serves 6

50 ml/2 fl oz vegetable or sunflower oil
50 g/1¾ oz butter
4 onions, halved and finely sliced
3 garlic cloves, crushed
1 kg/2 lb 3 oz medium white potatoes,
    peeled and diced into 2.5-cm/1-inch
    chunks
1 green chilli, finely chopped
70 g/2½ oz fresh coriander (cilantro)
    leaves, chopped
2 eggs
sea salt and freshly ground black
    pepper

This stew is vibrant with both flavour and texture, which is sure to make it an instant favourite. The potatoes are cooked until tender and fluffy inside, but deliciously crisp on the outside. Equally at home on both the breakfast and the dinner table and great on its own or as an accompaniment to other dishes.

Place the oil and butter in a large pan over a medium heat. Once the butter is melted and bubbling, add the onions and garlic and fry for 10 minutes, until tender and just starting to turn golden. Add the potatoes to the pan and stir to combine with the onion mixture. Add 100 ml/3½ fl oz water to the pan, bring to a simmer, covered, and leave to cook until the potatoes are almost tender, about 10 minutes. When the potatoes are almost cooked, add the chilli and most of the coriander (cilantro) and stir to combine. Add 200 ml/7 fl oz water.

Crack the eggs into a small bowl and beat with 1 tablespoon of water. Pour the egg mixture over the top of the potatoes and leave until they have coloured and are starting to bubble. Stir to break up the eggs and combine with the potato mixture, and continue to stir until the eggs are cooked through. Season to taste.

Serve the potato stew hot, garnished with the remaining coriander.

Tarkhunis Perogi
-TARRAGON PIE-

Preparation time: 40 minutes,
    plus 2 hours' resting time
Cooking time: 50 minutes
Serves 6–8

For the pastry:
1 tsp bicarbonate of soda
    (baking soda)
1 tbsp apple cider vinegar or white
    wine vinegar
500 g/1 lb 2 oz natural yogurt
2 eggs and 2 egg yolks
100 g/3½ oz butter, melted
600 g/1 lb 5 oz plain (all-purpose)
    flour

For the filling:
150 g/5½ oz butter
2 onions, chopped
3 bunches fresh tarragon
    (approximately 450 g/1 lb), leaves
    chopped
2 bunches spring onions (scallions),
    chopped
3 hard-boiled eggs, diced
sea salt and freshly ground black
    pepper

For glazing:
1 egg yolk, beaten
1 tsp olive oil
1 tbsp whole milk

Picking the tarragon leaves for this pie is a bit of a labour of love, but more than worth the effort in the end. The intense flavour of tarragon is paired with delicate and creamy boiled eggs, making it filling and packed with flavour. The oil in the glaze adds shine to the pastry and the milk keeps it soft. Because the filling is wrapped in pastry, this is also easy to eat on the go.

To make the pastry, mix together the bicarbonate of soda (baking soda), vinegar and yogurt in a large bowl. Add the eggs and egg yolk and whisk to combine. Add the melted butter and whisk again. Sift over the flour and bring together to form a soft dough. Knead the dough gently then cover and set aside in a warm place to rest for 2 hours.

Meanwhile, prepare the filling. Place the butter in a frying pan (skillet) over a medium heat. Once melted and bubbling, add the onions and cook, stirring continuously, for 10 minutes, until soft and translucent. Remove the pan from the heat and stir through all of the other filling ingredients. Set aside for 2 hours to allow the flavours to develop.

Preheat the oven to 180°C/350°F/gas mark 4 and ready a 30 x 40cm/12 x 16-inch baking dish.

Once the pastry has rested, divide it into 2 pieces, one slightly larger than the other. Working on a lightly floured surface, roll out the larger portion of pastry to line the base and sides of your dish. Spoon the filling into the pastry base. Mix together the ingredients for glazing and brush the edges of the pastry with the mixture.

Roll out the remaining pastry to fit over the top of the pie, then crimp the edges together and trim any excess pastry. Snip 2 small holes in the top of the pie and brush the pastry with the remaining glaze mixture just before baking.

Transfer the pie to the preheated oven to bake for 30–40 minutes, until golden. Serve hot.

Pomidori Tkhilit

-BAKED TOMATOES WITH HAZELNUTS-

Preparation time: 25 minutes
Cooking time: 45 minutes
Serves 6–8

2 tbsp olive oil
1kg/2lb 4 oz tomatoes, ripe but not
　soft
2 onions, halved and finely sliced
75g/2¾oz/½ cup hazelnuts
4 garlic cloves
1 tsp dried coriander (cilantro)
1 red chilli, finely chopped, or to taste
1 small handful parsley, leaves
　chopped, plus extra to garnish
1 small handful fresh coriander
　(cilantro), leaves chopped, plus
　extra to garnish

Beautifully sweet tomatoes, herbs pungent with summer and an underlying chilli note combine in this delicious side dish to make something that will elevate the plainest piece of grilled fish or meat into something very special.

Place 1 tablespoon of the oil in the base of a large pan, then lay the tomatoes over, fitting snugly in one layer. Cover the pan and place over a low heat for 5–10 minutes, until the tomatoes are slightly swollen and their skins have split.

Remove the tomatoes from the pan and peel off and discard their skins. Slice the tomatoes into quarters and set aside.

Heat the remaining oil in a large frying pan or skillet over a medium heat. Once hot, add the onions and cook, stirring continuously, until soft and just starting to turn golden, around 15 minutes. Add the tomatoes to the pan and continue to cook, stirring, for another 10 minutes. Take of the heat and set aside.

Place the hazelnuts in a food processor and process to a coarse, wet paste. Add the garlic, ground coriander, chilli and fresh herbs and pulse again to just combine.

Add the hazelnut paste to the pan with the tomatoes and return to the heat. Cook over a low heat, stirring continuously, for 10 minutes to allow the flavours to develop. Transfer to a serving platter and garnish with the fresh herbs. Serve hot.

Pomidori Kverzkhit

-BAKED TOMATOES AND EGGS-

Preparation time: 25 minutes
Cooking time: 45 minutes
Serves 6–8

2 tbsp olive oil
1kg/2lb 4 oz tomatoes, ripe but not
    soft
4 garlic cloves, crushed
5 eggs, beaten
1 bunch fresh basil, leaves torn
1 bunch fresh oregano, leaves picked
2 spring onions (scallions), finely
    sliced
sea salt and freshly ground pepper

This tomato and egg side dish is traditionally served at breakfast time and can be spooned over toast. I love it at any time of day, but it is especially delicious for a lazy weekend brunch. This is one of the most popular breakfast dishes at my Hackney-based café.

Place 1 tablespoon of the oil in the base of a large pan, then lay the tomatoes over, fitting snugly in one layer. Cover the pan and place over a low heat for 5–10 minutes, until the tomatoes are slightly swollen and their skins have split.

Remove the tomatoes from the pan and peel off and discard their skins. Slice the tomatoes into quarters and set aside.

Heat the remaining oil in a large frying pan (skillet) over a medium heat. Once hot, add the onions and cook, stirring continuously, until soft and just starting to turn golden, around 10 minutes.

Add the garlic, then the beaten eggs to the pan and cook until scrambled. Add the tomatoes, basil and oregano and cook over a low heat, stirring continuously, for 10 minutes to allow the flavours to develop. Transfer to a serving platter and garnish with the fresh herbs and spring onions. Serve hot.

Right: My father and grandmother.

Fruit Dishes

-CHAPTER 9-

Aladebi

Waking up to breakfast pancakes

Pancakes were always a highlight of mornings at home. On weekends, I used to go to sleep very late because I loved to watch the lights from the houses of the city slowly turn off one by one. During the day, the sights, smells and sounds of the city could almost swallow you, but at night, for a brief few hours, you were finally able to be alone. I remember, after one late night, being woken in the morning by the dappled sunlight on my face that was creeping into my room through the leaves of a large tree that stood beyond my balcony. Still half asleep, I could hear my mother's hushed voice talking in the kitchen and smell the aroma of delicious pancakes cooking on the stove; sizzling in oil and slowly turning crispy and golden, ready to be laid down in snowy yogurt with honey and fruit. I remember the excitement and the amazing feeling of expectation that the smell gave me – the best possible start to a fresh new day, with every possibility that something incredible could happen in the hours ahead.

Aladebi

-BREAKFAST PANCAKES-

Preparation time: 10 minutes,
   plus resting
Cooking time: 20 minutes
Makes 20

2 eggs
100 g/3½ oz caster (superfine) sugar
150 g/5½ oz/¾ cup low-fat natural
   yogurt mixed with 100 g/3½ oz/½
   cup crème fraîche or sour cream
¼ tsp lemon salt
200 g/7 oz plain (all-purpose) flour
   mixed with 50 g/2 oz potato starch
½ tsp bicarbonate of soda (baking
   soda)
100 ml/3½ fl oz vegetable oil, for
   frying

Topping suggestions (optional):
honey
yogurt
chopped nuts
fresh fruit
jam (jelly)

Growing up, these pancakes were always on the table at weekend breakfasts and I still associate them with relaxing mornings at the end of a busy week. They puff up during cooking and their texture is beautifully light and soft, somewhere between a doughnut and a pancake.

In a large bowl, beat the eggs and sugar together until pale and fluffy. Add the yogurt and crème fraîche mixture and lemon salt and whisk to combine. Set aside.

Sift the flour and potato starch mixture and bicarbonate of soda (baking soda) into another bowl and make a well in the centre. Pour the wet ingredients into the dry ingredients and whisk together until smooth. Leave to rest for 10 minutes.

Heat a large frying pan (skillet) over a medium heat and add the oil. Once hot, reduce the heat to low and spoon a small ladleful of the batter into the pan to form a pancake about 5 cm/2 inches across. Depending on the size of your pan, you can cook 2–3 pancakes at a time. Cover the pan and leave to cook for 2–3 minutes, until bubbles start to appear on the surface of the pancakes, then flip the pancakes and cook on the reverse side for 1 minute more. Keep warm while you cook the remaining pancakes.

Serve the pancakes warm with your choice of toppings.

Eteri's Vashlebi

-ETERI'S BAKED APPLE DUMPLINGS-

Preparation time: 20 minutes, plus at
    least 1 hour's resting time
Cooking time: 30 minutes
Serves 12

200 g/9 oz butter, at room temperature
350 g/12¼ oz/scant 2 cups plain (all-
    purpose) flour
½ tsp bicarbonate of soda (baking
    soda)
¼ tsp lemon salt
100 ml/3½ fl oz/scant ½ cup crème
    fraîche or sour cream
1 egg and 2 egg yolks, beaten
6 Golden Delicious apples
12 tsp brown sugar
2 tsp ground cinnamon (optional)
icing (confectioners') sugar, to serve

My aunt Eteri was renowned locally for her cakes and desserts. Whenever she came to visit she would also bring something sweet to enjoy over coffee and because of that I looked forward to her visits immensely. These baked apples enclosed in pastry are deliciously sweet, moist with apple and fragrant with earthy cinnamon.

Place the butter in a large bowl and sift over the flour and bicarbonate of soda (baking soda). Using your hands, rub the butter into the flour until the mixture resembles fine breadcrumbs.

Place the lemon salt in a small bowl and dissolve in a few drops of water. Place the crème fraîche or sour cream and dissolved lemon salt in a bowl or jug (pitcher) and stir to combine. Add the eggs to the flour and butter mixture and then pour in the lemon salt mixture, bringing it all together with your hands to form a smooth soft, dough. Wrap the dough in clingfilm (plastic wrap) and transfer to the fridge to rest for at least 1 hour or overnight.

An hour before you want to bake the dessert, remove the dough from the fridge, preheat the oven to 180°C/350°F/gas mark 4 and line a large baking sheet with parchment paper.

Peel the apples and slice in half horizontally, so that the core still runs through the centre of the apple halves. Using a sharp knife, remove the central core from the apples, being careful to stop before you cut right through the base. You should end up with 12 fillable apple cups.

On a lightly floured surface, roll the dough out to thickness of 5 mm/¼ inch. Using a large cutter or the base of a cake pan, cut 12 x 20-cm/8-inch circles from the dough, rolling and rerolling the scraps of dough as necessary.

Place an apple half in the centre of each dough circle and spoon 1 teaspoon of sugar into the centre of each apple. Sprinkle the cinnamon, if using, over the apples, and then bring up the edges of the dough and pinch them together to enclose the apples.

Transfer to the prepared baking sheet and place in the preheated oven for 30 minutes, until the pastry is golden and the apples are soft and juicy. Serve hot, sprinkled with icing (confectioners') sugar.

Eteri's Chitis Rdze

-ETERI'S CAKE-

Preparation time: 40 minutes, plus
    chilling overnight
Cooking time: 40 minutes
Serves 12

For the cake:
150 g/5 ½ oz butter, melted
400 g/14 oz/2 cups granulated sugar
1 tsp bicarbonate of soda (baking
    soda)
1 tbsp apple cider vinegar or white
    wine vinegar
400 g/14 oz/scant 2 cups low-fat
    natural yogurt
600 g/1 lb 5 oz/scant 6 cups plain (all-
    purpose) flour

For the cream:
150 g/5 ½ oz/1 cup plain (all-purpose)
    flour
2 tbsp potato starch
400 g/14 oz/2 cups granulated sugar
1 litre/1 ¾ pints/4 cups whole milk
200 g/7 oz butter, at room temperature

For the topping:
3 tbsp cocoa powder
5 tbsp granulated sugar
3 tbsp whole milk
50 g/1 ¾ oz butter, at room
    temperature

To assemble:
200 g/7 oz chopped walnuts
200 g/7 oz raisins

This is another of Eteri's famous cakes, and one that I often serve at the end of a meal because its sweetness is offset by the yogurt in the base, which gives a slight tartness to the end product. This looks beautiful on the table, so would also make a lovely birthday or celebration cake. This needs to be prepared the day before it is served.

Preheat the oven to 180°C/350°F/gas mark 4 and line four shallow 20-cm/8-inch cake pans with parchment paper.

To make the cake, place the butter and sugar in a large bowl and beat with an electric mixer until pale and well combined. Place the bicarbonate of soda (baking soda) in a small bowl and dissolve in the vinegar. Place the yogurt and dissolved bicarbonate of soda in a bowl or jug (pitcher) and stir to combine. Add this mixture to the sugar and butter mixture and stir to combine. Gradually sift the flour into this mixture, mixing between each addition. Once all of the flour has been added, knead to bring everything together into a thick dough. Divide the dough into 4 equal-sized pieces and press one piece into the base of each prepared cake pan, ensuring the base of the pans are well covered and the dough is evenly distributed. Transfer to the preheated oven for 10–15 minutes, until firm and golden. Transfer the cakes to wire racks to cool while you make the cream.

To make the cream, sift the flour and potato starch into a large bowl and add the sugar. Add enough of the milk to make a smooth paste, then set aside. Place the remaining milk in a large pan over a medium heat. Heat the milk until it just starts to bubble, then immediately remove from the heat and stir the flour paste into the milk. Return the pan to the heat and reduce the heat to low. Cook the mixture, stirring continuously, until the mixture is thick and is just starting to bubble. Remove from the heat and set aside until almost at room temperature. Once the cream has cooled, transfer to a mixing bowl and add the butter. Using an electric beater, beat the mixture until the butter is well combined. Set aside.

To make the topping, place the cocoa powder, sugar and milk in a small pan over a low heat. Whisk the mixture until just boiling, then remove from the pan and whisk in the butter. When the butter has melted, set aside.

To assemble the cake, place one-third of the cream on the bottom layer of the cake, using a spatula to spread the cream right to the edges. Scatter over one-third each of the walnuts and raisins and top with another layer of cake. Repeat this process until all of the cream filling, walnuts and raisins are used up, then top with the final layer of cake.

Pour the topping mixture over the top of the cake, using a hot knife to ensure and neat finish. Transfer the cake to the fridge overnight to set, then serve chilled from the fridge.

Deda's Shavi Kliavis Namzxvari

-DEDA'S PRUNE CAKE-

Preparation time: 30 minutes
Cooking time: 15 minutes
Serves 16

For the cake:
4 egg yolks
200 g/7 oz/1 cup caster (superfine)
  sugar
100 g/3½ oz butter, softened
1 tbsp sour cream
1 tsp bicarbonate of soda (baking
  soda)
1 tbsp apple cider vinegar or white
  wine vinegar
250 g/9 oz/2 cups plain (all-purpose)
  flour

For the filling:
300 g/10½ oz pitted prunes
100 g/3½ oz/½ cup caster (superfine)
  sugar
250 g/9 oz butter
500 ml/18 fl oz/2¼ cups sour cream
100 g/3½ oz/1 cup chopped roasted
  walnuts

Growing up, I would request this cake for my birthday every year and my friends would look forward to it with great anticipation. The sweetness of the jammy prune paste contrasts beautifully with the slight tang of the sour cream, giving this a slightly grown-up edge. Delicious with a cup of tea or coffee in the afternoon or as an elegant and impressive dinner-party dessert.

Preheat the oven to 200°C/400°F/gas mark 6 and grease 3 large baking sheets (measuring approximately 32 x 24 cm/12½ x 9½ inches) with butter and line with parchment paper.

To make the cake, place the egg yolks and sugar in a large bowl and beat with an electric whisk until pale and foamy. Add the butter and continue to beat until fully combined. Add the sour cream, bicarbonate of soda (baking soda) and vinegar and beat again to combine.

Sift the flour into the mixture and beat to bring together to form a firm dough. Divide the dough into three even pieces and press them into the bases of the prepared cake pans. Transfer to the oven to bake for 10 minutes, until golden and cooked through. Place on a wire rack to cool while you make the filling.

To make the filling, place the prunes in food processor with 4–5 tablespoons of water and pulse to a smooth, jammy paste.

Place the sugar, butter and sour cream in a large bowl and use an electric whisk to beat to combine. As soon as the mixture starts to come together and thicken, stop beating as the mixture can curdle if overworked. Add the prunes and most of the walnuts to the mixture and fold through to combine.

When the cake is cooled, slice off the edges and grate to create fine crumbs. Place one layer of the sponge on a serving plate and top with one-third of the filling mixture. Scatter over some of the remaining walnuts and cake crumbs and continue to build up the layers, finishing with a layer of filling. Transfer the cake to the fridge to set for a couple of hours before slicing.

Mamida's Alublis Namzxvari

-MAMIDA'S CHERRY CAKE-

Preparation time: 20 minutes
Cooking time: 35 minutes
Serves 12

3 eggs, beaten
375 g/13 oz/1¾ cups granulated sugar
1 tsp vanilla sugar
130 g/4½ oz/scant 1 cup sunflower oil,
    plus extra for greasing
½ tsp lemon salt
400 g/14 oz/1¾ cups crème fraîche or
    sour cream
100 g/3½ oz/scant ½ cup low-fat
    natural yogurt
525 g/1 lb 2½ oz/4¼ cups plain
    (all-purpose) flour
1 tsp bicarbonate of soda (baking
    soda)
pinch of salt
750 g/1 lb 10 oz/5 cups frozen cherries
ice cream or cream, to serve

My father's sister used to make this cake every year when cherries were in season and we all looked forward to it immensely. It's a simple recipe, but the cherries melt into the sponge while the cake cooks, making it wonderfully moist.

Preheat the oven to 180°C/350°F/gas mark 4 and grease a 33 x 22-cm (13 x 9-inch) cake pan with oil, line with parchment paper and grease again.

Place the eggs and granulated sugar in a large bowl and whisk until pale and fluffy. Add the vanilla sugar and oil and beat until smooth and well combined.

Place the lemon salt in a small bowl and dissolve in a few drops of water. Place the crème fraîche, yogurt and dissolved lemon salt in a large bowl or jug (pitcher) and stir to combine. Add this to the oil and egg mixture and beat until just combined.

Sift the flour, bicarbonate of soda (baking soda) and salt into the mixture and beat again until just combined.

Pour two-thirds of the cake batter into the cake pan and level out with a wooden spoon or spatula. Lay half of the frozen cherries over the cake batter in an even layer, then pour the remaining cake batter over the top to cover them. Lay the remaining cherries on top of the cake.

Bake in the preheated oven for 30–35 minutes, until the cake is golden, well risen and an inserted skewer comes out clean. This can be served warm or left to cool to room temperature before slicing. Serve with ice cream or cream.

Note: You can roll the frozen cherries in cornflour (cornstarch) before adding to the cake to help absorb some of the excess moisture.

Veta's Keksi

-VETA'S CAKE-

Preparation time: 20 minutes,
Cooking time: 35 minutes
Serves 12

200 g/7 oz butter, melted, plus extra
  for greasing
250 g/9 oz/1¼ cups granulated sugar
4 eggs
½ tsp lemon salt
300 g/10½ oz/1½ cups low-fat natural
  yogurt
100 g/3½ oz/scant ½ cup crème
  fraîche or sour cream
475 g/1 lb 1 oz/3½ cups plain (all-
  purpose) flour
1 tsp bicarbonate of soda (baking
  soda)
zest of ½ orange
1 tsp vanilla sugar
2 tbsp cocoa powder
icing (confectioners') sugar, to serve

This was a cake that was made by the grandmother of one of my childhood friends. I remember one winter when suddenly all our supplies were cut off and nothing was available in the shops. Despite these times of hardship, this cake was always on the table at my friend's house and even now a small slice can get me through the hardest of times.

Preheat the oven to 170°C/325°F/gas mark 3 and grease a large Bundt tin with butter.

Place the butter and sugar in the bowl of a stand mixer and mix on a medium speed until pale and well combined. With the mixer still running, crack in the eggs one at a time, allowing each egg to incorporate into the mixture before adding the next.

Place the lemon salt in a small bowl and dissolve in a few drops of water. Place the yogurt, crème fraîche or sour cream and dissolved lemon salt in a large bowl or jug (pitcher) and stir to combine. Add this mixture to the butter and egg mixture and beat until just combined.

Sift the flour and bicarbonate of soda (baking soda) into the mixture, then add the orange zest and vanilla sugar and beat again until just combined. Pour half the cake batter into a large bowl, leaving the remaining half in the bowl of the stand mixer. Sift the cocoa powder into the batter that is still in the bowl of the stand mixer and beat again until combined.

To create an attractive marble effect, gradually spoon cake batter from alternate bowls into the prepared Bundt tin, being careful not to be too heavy-handed as the two batters will mix together.

Transfer to the preheated oven to bake for 30 minutes, until the cake is golden, well risen and an inserted skewer comes out clean. Leave to cool for 10 minutes, then turn the cake out of its tin and leave to cool on a wire rack. Sprinkle with icing (confectioners') sugar before serving.

Khajos Namzxvari

-COTTAGE CHEESE CAKE WITH APRICOT-

Preparation time: 20 minutes
Cooking time: 35 minutes
Serves 16

300 g/10½ oz/2 cups plain (all-
    purpose) flour
½ tsp bicarbonate of soda (baking
    soda)
200 g/7 oz cold butter, coarsely grated
½ tsp sea salt
200 g/7 oz/scant 1 cup cottage cheese
200 g/7 oz/1 cup caster (superfine)
    sugar
500 g/1 lb 2 oz apricots, halved and
    pitted

For the topping:
1 egg
200 g/7 oz/1 cup caster (superfine)
    sugar
200 ml/7 fl oz/scant cup sour cream
½ tsp vanilla extract
2 tbsp plain (all-purpose) flour

This is not a cheesecake, but a cake made with cottage cheese in the batter. The cheese lifts the sponge and tempers the sweetness of the fruit and custard topping. If apricots aren't in season, you could use any stone fruit that is available.

Preheat the oven to 180°C/350°F/gas mark 4 and grease a loose-bottomed 25-cm/10-inch cake pan with butter.

Sift the flour and bicarbonate of soda (baking soda) into a large bowl, then add the butter, salt, cottage cheese, sugar and 1 teaspoon of water. Mix together to form a crumbly dough, then press into the base of the prepared cake pan.

Lay the apricot halves over the top of the cake mixture, pressing them slightly into the batter. Transfer to the preheated oven for 20–25 minutes, until golden.

Meanwhile, make the topping. In a large bowl, beat the egg with the sugar until pale and frothy. Add the sour cream, vanilla extract and flour and whisk until smooth. Pour this mixture over the cake and return to the oven for around 10 minutes, until set to a soft custard consistency.

Leave the cake to cool for 10 minutes before removing from its pan. It is delicious eaten warm or cooled to room temperature.

Nigvziani Ruleti

-WALNUT ROULADE-

Preparation time: 30 minutes,
    plus at least 1 hour's resting time
Cooking time: 30 minutes
Makes approximately 15 slices

200 g/7 oz butter, softened
475–500 g/1 lb 1 oz/3¾ cups plain
    (all-purpose) flour, plus extra for
    dusting
½ tsp bicarbonate of soda (baking
    soda)
200 g/7 oz/scant 1 cup crème fraîche
    or sour cream
50 g/2 oz/¼ cup low-fat yogurt
1 egg yolk
200 g/7 oz/scant 2 cups walnuts,
    roasted and coarsely ground
200 g/7 oz/1 cup caster
    (superfine) sugar
150 g/5½ oz/1 cup raisins, soaked until
    plump then drained (optional)
pinch of ground cinnamon
pinch of salt
icing (confectioners') sugar, to dust

Somewhere between a cake and cookie, this roulade is rich with the flavours of cinnamon and walnuts and makes an excellent mid-afternoon pick-me-up with a cup of coffee.

Preheat the oven to 180°C/350°F/gas mark 4 and line a large baking sheet with parchment paper.

Place the butter in a large bowl. Sift the flour and bicarbonate of soda (baking soda) into the bowl. Bring the mixture together with your hands to the consistency of fine breadcrumbs. Add the crème fraîche, yogurt and the egg yolk and bring the mixture together with your hands to a firm dough.

Divide the dough into 2 equal-size pieces, wrap in clingfilm (plastic wrap) and transfer to the fridge to rest for at least 1 hour.

Meanwhile, place the walnuts, sugar, raisins (if using), cinnamon and salt in a bowl and stir to combine.

Once the dough has rested, working with one piece of dough at a time, place the dough on a lightly floured surface and roll into a large rectangle measuring approximately 5-mm/¼-inch thick. Spread the sugar mixture over the surface of the dough, then, working from the widest edge of the dough rectangle, roll the dough into a long cylinder.

Transfer to the preheated oven to cook for 20–30 minutes, until golden and cooked through. Transfer to a wire rack to cool.

Dust with icing (confectioners') sugar just before serving and slice into portions.

Vashlis Perogi
-GEORGIAN APPLE PIE-

Preparation time: 20 minutes
Cooking time: 45 minutes
Serves 8

6 cooking apples, peeled, cored and
    cut into 1-cm/½-inch chunks
200 g/7 oz/1 cup plus 1 tsp granulated
    sugar
250 g/9 oz sunflower spread
1 tsp vanilla sugar
3 eggs
300 g/10½ oz/2¼ cups plain (all-
    purpose) flour
60 g/2¼ oz/½ cup potato flour
2 tsp bicarbonate of soda (baking
    soda)
250 g/9 oz/generous cup low-fat
    natural yogurt
1 tsp lemon salt, dissolved in a little
    cold water
double (heavy) cream or ice cream, to
    serve

Similar to an American cobbler, this delicious dessert is topped with a soft sponge on a bed of sweet apple purée. Warming and comforting, this is delicious served with ice cream or custard.

Preheat the oven to 180°C/350°F/gas mark 4 and grease a large rectangular cake pan (approximately 32 x 24 cm/12½ x 9½ inches) with oil and line with parchment paper.

Place the apple in a medium pan with enough water to cover the base of the pan and bring to a simmer over a low heat. Cook until the apples have broken down into a smooth purée and have taken on a light golden brown colour. Just before ready, add 1 teaspoon of sugar and the vanilla sugar. Set aside in the pan to cool.

Cream the sunflower spread and sugar together in a large bowl with an electric mixer, then add the eggs one and a time, beating with the mixer to combine between each addition.

In a separate bowl, sift both flours and the bicarbonate of soda (baking soda), then add the yogurt and lemon salt to the bowl and mix to combine.

Pour the flour and yogurt mixture into the bowl with the butter, sugar and eggs, then fold everything together until you have a smooth batter (do not use the electric mixer for this stage).

Pour the cake batter into your prepared cake pan and level the surface with a spatula. Pour the cooled apple purée over the batter, then use the spatula to gentle ripple it through the cake batter.

Transfer the cake to the oven and cook for 30 minutes, until golden and well risen. The cake is cooked when an inserted wooden skewer comes out clean — be careful when checking as the apple purée remains quite wet when the cake is cooked, so you are looking for residual cake batter only.

Slice the cake in the pan and transfer to serving plates. Serve hot with double (heavy) cream or ice cream.

Pelamushi

-GRAPE JELLIES-

Preparation time: 10 minutes,
  plus at least 3 hours for setting
Cooking time: 15 minutes
Makes 1 large or 6 small jellies

6 tbsp plain (all-purpose) flour
2 tbsp sugar
1 litre/4 cups 100% grape juice (dark)
roasted hazelnuts, to serve

These grape jellies are perhaps the most recognizable Georgian dessert and always go down well in the restaurant. They are set with flour rather than gelatine and need to be left for several hours to set. They look especially pretty if you use small decorative moulds.

Sift the flour into a small bowl and stir in 1 tablespoon of the sugar. Add a little of the grape juice and stir to make a loose paste.

Place three-quarters of the remaining grape juice in a pan over a medium heat. Pour in the paste and cook, stirring continuously, until just boiling, then reduce the heat to a simmer and continue to cook, still stirring, until thickened. Add the remaining sugar and grape juice to the pan and cook for around 8 minutes more — if the mixture is too thin, add a little more flour to thicken.

Transfer the mixture into individual moulds or serving glasses and place in the fridge for at least 3 hours to set. Serve scattered with roasted hazelnuts.

Glossary of Ingredients

Ajika
A spicy paste made of chillies, garlic, herbs and spices that is used to flavour food. *Ajika* can vary in colour between red and green, depending on what type of chilli is used as its base. *Ajika* is often stirred into soups, stews and sauces to add flavour and spice, but is also served alongside food as a condiment when you need a punch of chilli heat.

Bazha
A spiced walnut paste that forms the basis of many Georgian dishes. Walnuts are processed to a very smooth paste, flavoured with garlic and spices (often ground coriander, ground dried marigold and blue fenugreek) and diluted with vinegar and water. The sauce is often served with fried poussin or *Tabaka* (Spiced Pan-fried Poussin, see page 140).

Blue Fenugreek
One of the three spices (along with dried ground marigold and ground coriander) used to make the traditional Georgian spice mix or *suneli*. Similar in flavour to fenugreek, but with a milder flavour, Blue fenugreek grows wild in Georgia's mountainous north and both the seeds and pods of the plant are ground to produce the spice. Can be substituted with fenugreek.

Caul Fat
The thin lacy membrane that surrounds the internal organs of cows, sheep and pigs. It is often used to encase minced (ground) meat before frying; this adds flavour and ensures that the meat is stays moist during cooking.

Ground Dried Marigold see Marigold

Khachapuri
Georgian cheese bread that is usually served alongside the hot dishes at a *supra*. Each region of Georgia has its own specialty, with toppings and fillings ranging from mashed potato, boiled eggs and even meat.

Kharcho Suneli
A traditional spice mix that is used to flavour *kharcho*-type (see below) dishes. Usually a mix of equal parts ground coriander, blue fenugreek and ground dried marigold, in Georgian kitchens, jars of this mix will be ready made up and ready to add to food during cooking.

Kharcho
A rich soup or stew with a walnut sauce and *kharcho suneli* (see above) at its base. One of Georgia's most famous exports, beef *kharcho* is the most widely known, though versions using pork, lamb, chicken and vegetarian varieties are also popular.

Khinkali
Dumplings filled with spiced meats or cheeses. *Khinkhali* are recognisable through their delicate accordion-fold construction and central dough stalk. They are eaten by picking the dumpling up by its stalk and biting off the base.

Lavash
Large unleavened flatbreads, often rectangular in shape. In Georgia, these are often filled with meat and salads before rolling and eating. Tortilla wraps make a good substitute.

Lobio
A traditional Georgian dish made up of various kinds of dried or canned bean. There are many variations of *lobio*, both hot and cold.

Marigold
The dried and ground petals of the marigold flower are revered in Georgia for their earthy flavour and attractive autumnal hue. The flavour has a slight metallic tang that is similar to saffron, which could be used as a substitute.

Pomegranate Molasses
A concentrated syrup made from pomegranate juice. The flavour is both intensely sweet and sour and so should be used sparingly. Can be added to dishes or used as a sauce in its own right.

Potato Starch
Starch derived from potatoes, often used to absorb moisture. Used in cake baking, potato starch helps to achieve soft and moist sponges.

Sour Green Plums
These cherry-sized plums are bright in colour and have a refreshingly trat and crunchy flavour. When used in sauces, the plums melt down and impart and delicious sour undertone. Can be substituted with lime juice.

Sulguni
Traditional Georgian brined cheese with a salty flavour. Because of importation laws, it is very hard to locate in the UK, but mozzarella and halloumi make acceptable substitutes.

Supra
A traditional Georgian feast, taking place over the course of many hours with many courses of food interspersed by toasting, speeches, drinking and music. (See pages 9–11 for more details).

Tamada
The toastmaster of a *supra* who is nominated by the host family, though often not a member of that family. In charge of proposing toasts and regaling the assembled guests with stories and anecdotes to drive the event forward.

Suppliers

UK

Amazon
www.amazon.co.uk
Online marketplace and useful resource for hard-to-find ingredients, including dried herbs, edible flowers and spices.

Caucasian Spice Box
www.caucasians.co.uk
Online store stocking Georgian spices, including ground marigold, blue fenugreek, summer savory and ready-made *ajikas*. Distributes throughout the UK.

The Georgian Wine Society
www.georgianwinesociety.co.uk
+44 (0) 7946 262498
Online retailer of fine Georgian wines, selling wine by the half or full case. Also offers specially curated mixed cases for those looking for a good cross section. Delivery throughout the UK.

Marani Wine
www.marani.co
Our wine supplier at Little Georgia.

Natoora
www.natoora.co.uk
+44 (0)20 7237 0346
Fresh fruit, vegetables, cheese and deli foods available for home delivery.

Sous Chef
www.souschef.co.uk
+44 (0)20 8340 2139
Online resource for adventurous home cooks, offering ingredients and equipment inspired by leading chefs and international cuisines.

The Spice Shop
thespiceshop.co.uk
+44 (0)20 7221 4448
+44 (0)1273 911464
London and Brighton-based shop with good range of spices. Spices are available for delivery nationwide through online store.

Waitrose
www.waitrose.com
+44 (0)1344 825 232
Supermarket with locations nationwide, selling high-quality food and drink. Stockists of a wide range of fresh and dried herbs and spices and other quality food products.

Whole Foods Market
www.wholefoodsmarket.com
+44 (0)20 7368 6100
High-quality natural and organic foods, including fresh fruit and vegetables, committed to sustainable agriculture.

US

Bazaar Spices
www.bazaar spices.com
+1 (202) 379 2907
A Washington-based store with online shop selling a good range of dried herbs and spices, including ground marigold and blue fenugreek. Ships nationwide.

Georgian Gourmet
www.georgiangourmet.com
+1 (988) 531 9888
Online store with a good range of spices and ready-made sauces. Delivers nationwide.

Georgian Wine House
www.georgianwinehouse.com
+1 (301) 931 0030
Importer of Georgian wines that sells into stores nationwide. Website includes a state-by-state search to find stockists of Georgian wine in your area.

Whole Foods Market
www.wholefoodsmarket.com
+1 (844) 936 2273
High-quality natural and organic foods, including fresh fruit and vegetables, committed to sustainable agriculture.

AUS

Herbie's Spices
www.herbies.com.au
+61 (02) 4392 9422
Online store selling a good range of dried herbs and spices, including summer savory. Ships nationwide.

Tamada
www.tamada.com.au
+61 (02) 8739 7247
Importer of Georgian wines with online store selling wines by the bottle, half case or case. Ships nationwide.

Index

This book is dedicated to all those who came into my life and left the gift of sweet memories. I thank you.

I would like to thank all at Pavilion who supported this book and made it possible. To Krissy Mallett who first approached me, Katie Cowan and Stephanie Milner who helped throughout. Great thanks also go to Dan Hurst for his patience with my English, Valerie Berry and Alex James Gray who brought the recipes to life, Yuki Sugiura for her beautiful photographs, Alexander Breeze for filling the photographs with such lovely things and Laura Russell for framing everything so beautifully with her design. Thanks also to Sophie Yamamoto who pulled it all together.

I owe a huge debt to my mother who inspired most of the recipes, Tamara Melikishvili, my sister–in–law, who provided illustrations for the book, and Nina Anjaparidze, Zaira Chantladze and Clive Crotty who supplied images of Georgia.

Special thanks must also go to Eldar Shengelaia who provided posters of his movies for inclusion in these pages and Natalia Jughedi for making that possible.

Right: Me as a child in Georgia.